Credit and General COMPUTING STUDIES

The National Qualifications Examination Papers and the
Scottish Certificate of Education Examination Papers
are reprinted by special permission of
THE SCOTTISH QUALIFICATIONS AUTHORITY

ISBN 0 7169 9328 7
© *Robert Gibson & Sons, Glasgow, Ltd., 2000.*

The answers to the questions do not emanate from the Authority.
They reflect the author's opinion of what might be expected in the
Standard Grade Computing Studies Examination.

ROBERT GIBSON · Publisher
17 Fitzroy Place, Glasgow, G3 7SF.

1996
MONDAY, 20 MAY
10.50 AM – 12.05 PM

COMPUTING STUDIES
STANDARD GRADE
General Level

Read each question carefully.

Attempt **all** questions.

Write your answers in the space provided on the question paper.

Write as neatly as possible.

Answer in sentences wherever possible.

Before leaving the examination room you must give this book to the Invigilator. If you do not, you may lose all the marks for this paper.

CONTENTS

KU | PS

1. John works in the office of a garage.

The garage uses a computer and a database package to hold information about customers and their cars.

Here is the information held about one of the customers.

Name	Smith J
Street	5 Holdsworth Crescent
Town	Townside
Tel No	0141 635 2437
Next Service Due	November 1996
Car–Make & Model	Ford Fiesta
Reg No	P294 RFY

(a) Describe how John could use the database package to get a list of all customers in alphabetical order.

_____

_____

_____

2
1
0

(b) The garage is going to offer a special price to service Volkswagen Polo cars in June 1996.

Describe how John could use the database package to obtain a list of all customers with Volkswagen Polo cars which are due to be serviced in June 1996.

_____

_____

_____

_____

3
2
1
0

	KU	PS

(c) Some customers are very concerned that information about them is being kept on a computer.

  (i) Describe **two** concerns they may have.

    1 _____

    _____

    2 _____

    _____

2
1
0

  (ii) What could the garage do to reassure the customers about these concerns?

    1 _____

    _____

    2 _____

    _____

2
1
0

(d) The garage used to keep the information about customers on cards.

Give **two** advantages of using the database package instead of cards.

1 _____

_____

2 _____

_____

2
1
0

4

	KU	PS

2. Maureen is using the word processing section of an integrated package to produce her Modern Studies report.

(a) She decides that the second paragraph should actually be at the end of the report.

How could Maureen use the software to make this change without re-typing the paragraph?

_____

_____

_____

1
0

(b) Maureen has used a spell checker on her report.

Describe **two** limitations of a spell checker.

1 _____

_____

2 _____

_____

2
1
0

(c) Maureen is worried that a disc fault will mean that she will have to re-type her report.

Describe fully what she should do to make sure that if there is a disc fault she will not have to re-type her report.

_____

_____

_____

_____

2
1
0

5

	KU	PS

(d) Maureen uses the spreadsheet section of the integrated package to produce a table of figures.

She then includes this table in her word processed report.

Give **two** advantages of using an integrated package rather than separate packages to produce her report.

1 _____

_____

2 _____

_____

2
1
0

(e) Maureen uses the graphics section of the integrated package to produce some drawings.

Her teacher suggests that she could use the *scale graphic* feature to alter one of her drawings.

What effect would using the scale graphic feature have on her drawing?

_____

_____

_____

1
0

(f) Maureen wishes to include a photograph in the report.

She decides to use a scanner to include the photograph in her report rather than to stick the photograph onto her report.

Give **one** advantage of scanning the photograph rather than sticking it onto the report.

_____

_____

_____

1
0

	KU	PS

3. (*a*) Drawplan Architects uses a Computer Aided Design (CAD) system to draw up detailed building plans.

    (i) Give **two** advantages of using a CAD system to draw the plans rather than drawing them by hand.

       1 _____

       _____

       2 _____

       _____

KU: 2 1 0

    (ii) What output device should be used to produce the CAD plans?

       _____

KU: 1 0

    (iii) Before the CAD system was introduced, the plans were drawn by hand.

       Give **two** possible effects that the CAD system may have on the workforce of Drawplan Architects.

       1 _____

       _____

       2 _____

       _____

PS: 2 1 0

(*b*) A computer is used to control the central heating in the offices of Drawplan Architects. Each office has a temperature sensor linked to the computer.

The computer uses *closed loop* control.

    (i) What is meant by closed loop control?

       _____

       _____

       _____

KU: 2 1 0

    (ii) Why is closed loop control used for this system?

       _____

       _____

PS: 1 0

	KU	PS

(iii) When the computer controlled central heating system was first installed, the offices were always too hot.

Suggest what was done at the computer to reduce the temperature in the offices.

_____

_____

2
1
0

(iv) Suggest **two** other ways in which the computer could be used to control the office environment.

1 _____

_____

2 _____

_____

2
1
0

KU PS

4. Donald lives on an island. He owns a boat and uses it to transport passengers from the island to the nearest town.

Here is part of the spreadsheet which he uses to keep a record of his expenses and income.

	A	B	C	D	E	F
1	COSTS (in £s)		JANUARY	FEBRUARY	MARCH	APRIL
2	Diesel Oil		100·00	120·00	125·00	115·00
3	Repairs		50·00	30·00	40·00	35·00
4	Pier Charges		10·00	15·00	20·00	15·00
5	Insurance		15·00	17·00	17·50	17·00
6	TOTAL COSTS		175·00	182·00	202·50	182·00
7						
8	PASSENGER FARES		420·00	500·20	525·45	480·80
9						
10	PROFIT		245·00	318·20	322·95	298·80

(a) Cells C6 and C10 each contain a formula.

   (i) Suggest a suitable formula for cell C6.

   _____

1
0

   (ii) Suggest a suitable formula for cell C10.

   _____

1
0

(b) The formula in C6 has been replicated across to the other cells in row 6.

   Where else in the spreadsheet above could the replicate feature have been used?

   _____

   _____

   _____

2
1
0

	KU	PS

(c) Donald decides to pay a friend £50·00 a month to collect the fares from the passengers. He wants to include this cost in the spreadsheet.

Describe how this can be done.

_____

_____

_____

2
1
0

(d) The spreadsheet package Donald is using has a *human computer interface* (HCI) which is *command driven*.

(i) What is meant by the term human computer interface (HCI)?

_____

_____

_____

1
0

(ii) Give **one** advantage of a command driven HCI.

_____

_____

_____

1
0

	KU	PS

5. Shereen works on a nature reserve. Her job involves collecting data about birds.

(*a*) Her employers gave her a palmtop computer which uses handwriting recognition to help her collect the data.

Why might Shereen find this type of computer particularly useful?

_____

_____

PS **10**

(*b*) When Shereen returns to her house she is able to transfer the data she has collected onto her desktop computer.

She then produces a report and sends it electronically to her employers.

What additional device does Shereen have to send reports in this way?

_____

KU **10**

(*c*) Shereen is able to work from home using her computer.

   (i) Give **two** advantages for Shereen of being able to work from home.

     1 _____

     _____

     2 _____

     _____

PS **210**

  (ii) Give **one** advantage for Shereen's employers if Shereen works at home.

     _____

PS **10**

11

	KU	PS

(*c*) (iii) If more people were to work from home using computers, this could have widespread effects on society.

Give **two** possible effects on society if more people were to work in this way.

1 _____

_____

2 _____

_____

**2
1
0**

	KU	PS

6. Quickshop is a supermarket.

The customers' purchases are entered using a bar code reader at point of sale terminals.

(*a*) (i) Give **two** advantages of entering the purchases using a bar code reader rather than by typing in the prices.

1 _____

_____

2 _____

_____

2
1
0

(ii) Part of the bar code represents a *check digit*.

What is a check digit and why is it used?

_____

_____

_____

_____

2
1
0

(*b*) Once the bar code has been read at the point of sale terminal, the information is processed and a customer receipt is printed.

This is an example of *interactive processing*.

(i) What is meant by interactive processing?

_____

_____

_____

1
0

(ii) Why is interactive processing used here?

_____

_____

_____

1
0

| | KU | PS |

(*c*) The customer pays by using electronic funds transfer at point of sale (EFTPOS).

The customer gives his bank card to the shop assistant. The bank details are read from the card.

   (i) The customer must then use a small keypad to enter his personal identification number (PIN).

       Why is a personal identification number (PIN) necessary?

       _____

       _____

1
0

  (ii) Before the customer leaves with the shopping the shop must be satisfied that it will receive payment.

       How does the shop know if the customer has enough money in his account?

       _____

       _____

       _____

2
1
0

	KU	PS

(d) Quickshop uses *batch processing* to process its payroll.

    (i) What is meant by batch processing?

_____

_____

_____

2
1
0

    (ii) Give **one** advantage for Quickshop of using batch processing.

_____

_____

_____

1
0

(e) Quickshop employs data preparation operators and computer operators in the payroll department.

    (i) Describe **one** task that data preparation operators would do as part of their job.

_____

_____

1
0

    (ii) Describe **one** task that computer operators would do as part of their job.

_____

_____

1
0

		KU	PS

7. (*a*) All computers need to have an operating system.

State **two** tasks an operating system would carry out.

1 _____

_____

2 _____

_____

2
1
0

(*b*) Describe **one** difference between a program written in a high level computer language and a program written in machine code.

_____

_____

_____

_____

1
0

(*c*) Computers can process many types of data including graphics and text.

(i) Below is a small computer graphic. Each square is either black or white. The computer uses a Ø to represent a white square and a 1 to represent a black square.

The computer represents the first four rows of the graphic as shown in the grid below.

Ø	Ø	1	Ø	Ø	1	Ø	Ø
Ø	1	Ø	1	1	1	1	Ø
1	Ø	Ø	Ø	Ø	Ø	Ø	1
1	Ø	Ø	Ø	Ø	Ø	Ø	1

Complete the grid above to show how the last two rows of the graphic are represented.

(ii) How many bytes would it take to store this graphic?

_____

2
1
0

1
0

(*d*) Different printers can have different *character sets*.

What is meant by a character set?

_____

1
0

[END OF QUESTION PAPER]

COMPUTING STUDIES
STANDARD GRADE
General Level

Read each question carefully.

Attempt **all** questions.

Write your answers in the space provided on the question paper.

Write as neatly as possible.

Answer in sentences wherever possible.

Before leaving the examination room you must give this book to the invigilator. If you do not, you may lose all the marks for this paper.

KU	PS

1. Grant Electrical is a company which sells video systems.

   The Company uses a database package to hold information about customers and their purchases.

   Here is one of the records in the database.

Name	Henderson J	Date of Purchase	5 May 1997
Address	5 Main Street	Make	Sunny
	Aytown	Model	Triton 567
	Beshire		
Post code	BE04 7YC		

(a) The Company wishes to have a list of all customers in alphabetical order.

   Describe how you could use the database to list all customers in alphabetical order.

   _____

   _____

   _____

2
1
0

(b) The Company is offering a special price on new Sunny videos. They wish to write to customers who bought Sunny videos more than three years ago.

   On which **two** fields do they need to search?

   Field 1: _____

   Field 2: _____

2
1
0

	KU	PS

(c) The customer's details are entered at a computer in the shop when a video is bought. The details are then transferred using a telephone line to a computer at the head office of Grant Electrical.

  (i) What type of network is used by Grant Electrical?

  _____

KU 1 0

  (ii) Describe **two** other ways in which the Company could make use of this network.

  1 _____

  _____

  2 _____

  _____

PS 2 1 0

(d) Grant Electrical sometimes sells lists of customer details to other companies.

  (i) Give **one** advantage to Grant Electrical of selling these customer lists.

  _____

  _____

PS 1 0

  (ii) Give **one** advantage for a company which buys these customer lists.

  _____

  _____

PS 1 0

  (iii) Some customers do not want to be on these customer lists.
  Give **one** reason why they may **not** want to be on these customer lists.

  _____

  _____

PS 1 0

KU | PS

2. Autobus Tours is a company providing bus services and tour holidays throughout the country.

A spreadsheet is used to store information about each bus service.

The TOTAL COSTS and PROFIT are calculated automatically using formulae.

Part of the spreadsheet is shown below.

	A	B	C	D	E
1		Autobus Tours		January 1997	
2					
3	**Bus Service Number**	**23**	**57**	**79**	**113**
4					
5	Number of Passengers	156	3023	509	2053
6					
7	PASSENGER FARES	£702·00	£2569·55	£875·48	£3012·67
8					
9	Diesel	£67·50	£87·56	£97·67	£103·56
10	Wages	£480·00	£960·80	£480·40	£960·80
11	Repairs/Servicing	£159·00	£50·00	£60·00	£50·00
12	TOTAL COSTS	£706·50	£1098·36	£638·07	£1114·36
13					
14	PROFIT	−£4·50	£1471·19	£237·41	£1898·31

(a) The PROFIT for each bus service is calculated by taking the TOTAL COSTS away from the PASSENGER FARES.

Suggest a suitable formula for cell C14.

1
0

(b) All the formulae needed to calculate the TOTAL COSTS for each bus service may be *replicated* from the formula in cell B12.

What happens when a formula is replicated?

2
1
0

KU | PS

(c) The data for cell C10 was displayed as 960·8 when it was entered.

What has been done to the cell attributes to change the way the data appears?

_____

_____

_____

1
0

(d) A new bus service, number 48, is to be introduced. Details about bus service number 48 must be entered so that the bus service numbers are in increasing order.

Describe what must be done to the spreadsheet to enter the details about the new service.

_____

_____

2
1
0

(e) Passengers can access up-to-date information about bus services in the bus station by touching the appropriate words on a screen, as shown below.

(i) What type of input device is being used?

_____

1
0

(ii) Give **one** advantage of using this type of input device here.

_____

1
0

	KU	PS

(f) When a customer books a holiday with Autobus Tours, they are asked to list their interests.

The Company uses a word processing package and *standard paragraphs* to produce a suitable information sheet for each individual customer.

   (i) Give **two** advantages of using standard paragraphs to produce an information sheet for each customer.

1 _____

_____

2 _____

_____

2
1
0

   (ii) The word processing package is *command driven*.

Give **one** advantage of using a command driven package rather than a menu driven package.

_____

1
0

(g) The use of the computer will involve *running costs*.

Give **two** examples of computer running costs.

1 _____

_____

2 _____

_____

2
1
0

3. Alan works for a company which owns a chain of shops.

Each month the directors of the company hold a meeting with the shop managers.

Part of Alan's job is to attend the meetings and to write a report on what happened at each meeting.

He uses a word processing package and printer to produce each report.

(a) Alan used to write the report by hand.

Give **two** advantages of using a word processing package and printer to produce a report.

1 _____

_____

2 _____

_____

KU
2 1 0

(b) The word processing package includes a *spelling check* feature.

(i) How does the spelling check feature help Alan to find and correct his spelling mistakes?

_____

_____

_____

_____

_____

KU
2 1 0

(ii) Describe **one** type of spelling error which may not be discovered by the spelling check feature.

_____

_____

_____

KU
1 0

(iii) The spelling check feature highlights some words which are not spelling errors.

Explain why this happens.

_____

_____

KU
1 0

23

	KU	PS

(c) This month's report fills one page and a small part of the next page.

Describe how Alan could use the word processing package to alter the layout so that the report only uses one page.

_____

_____

_____

_____

1
0

(d) Alan also writes articles for the company newsletter.

He attends the opening of a new shop. He uses a palmtop computer to make notes to help him write an article for the newsletter.

(i) Why does Alan find a palmtop computer useful for this task?

_____

_____

1
0

(ii) Tick the box below which describes the input method Alan is using.

keyboard ☐   mouse ☐

voice recognition ☐   handwriting recognition ☐

1
0

(iii) The palmtop computer uses an LCD output.

What do the letters LCD stand for?

_____

1
0

	KU	PS

(iv) The new shop is in Newtown. The name of the town appears many times in the article. Unfortunately, in the article, Alan said that the shop was in Newport.

(A) Describe how Alan could use the word processing package to find and correct these mistakes quickly and easily.

_____

_____

_____

(B) Alan uses the *on-line help* facility to remind him of how to correct this kind of mistake.

What is meant by on-line help?

_____

_____

_____

KU: 1 0

PS: 1 0

	KU	PS

4. Joanne lives in Aceton where a committee has been set up to raise funds for a new swimming pool.

The committee is running a competition to design a logo.

(*a*) Joanne decides to use a new graphics package to design a logo for the competition.

The package has an *on-line tutorial*.

What is an on-line tutorial?

_____

_____

2
1
0

(*b*) Joanne designs the following logo.

Name or describe **two** of the graphic tools which Joanne has used to produce the logo.

1 _____

_____

2 _____

_____

1
0

(*c*) Joanne then decides to alter the logo as shown below.

Describe **two** features of the graphics package which Joanne has used to make these changes.

1 _____

_____

2 _____

2
1
0

_____

	KU	PS

(d) Joanne's entry wins the competition.

The swimming pool committee decides to use Joanne's logo.

Joanne's disc cannot be read by the committee's computer.

What device could the committee use to input the logo from Joanne's printed copy?

_____

10 (PS)

(e) The committee uses the word processing section of an integrated package to write its letters. The letters have to include the logo from the graphics section.

Give **one** advantage of using an integrated package rather than separate graphics and word processing packages to include the logo on the letter.

_____

_____

_____

10 (PS)

(f) The swimming pool committee stores information about its members in the database section of the integrated package.

Some members are concerned that this information could be misused.

Give **one** step that the swimming pool committee could take to make sure that the information is not misused.

_____

_____

10 (PS)

KU | PS

5. Heavycar Manufacture is a company which assembles cars. Heavycar Manufacture uses robots to move car parts from one part of the factory to another.

car parts

robot

magnetic guide

(a) The robot shown above is using a magnetic guide to move from one part of the factory to another.

How does the robot detect the magnetic guide?

_____

_____

1
0

(b) The computer controlling the robot uses *closed loop* control.

Explain what is meant by the term closed loop.

_____

_____

2
1
0

(c) Employees of Heavycar Manufacture are concerned about accidents which could be caused by robots moving around the factory floor.

Suggest **two** safety precautions which would guard against people being injured by the robots.

1 _____

_____

2 _____

_____

2
1
0

	KU	PS

(d) Heavycar Manufacture also uses stationary robots to do jobs in the car factory.

One job is to spray cars with paint. The spray painting used to be carried out by humans.

Describe **two** advantages of using robots to spray the cars.

1 _____

_____

2 _____

_____

2
1
0

(e) Parts of the car have to be joined together by welding. Heavycar Manufacture wishes to use the stationary robots to weld these parts of the car together.

What would have to be done to the **computer** controlling the stationary robots?

_____

_____

1
0

(f) Some employees of Heavycar Manufacture feel that their jobs have changed since the robots were introduced.

Describe how the use of robots could **improve** working conditions for the factory employees.

_____

_____

1
0

	KU	PS

6. (*a*) Customers of the Highlife Bank can use automated telling machines to obtain cash. Each customer has a special bank card.

When customers use their bank card to obtain money, they are asked to use a small keypad to enter a code.

Explain why they are asked to enter this code.

_____

_____

1
0

(*b*) Customers can also use their cheque book to obtain cash inside any bank.

special
characters

What is the name given to the special type of characters printed on cheques as labelled in the above diagram?

_____

1
0

(*c*) Jagheer is a customer of Highlife Bank. He goes to a shop to buy a pair of dungarees for his daughter.

He takes the dungarees to the sales assistant who uses a reader to read the tag on the dungarees.

(i) What is the name given to this type of input?

_____

1
0

	KU	PS

(ii) The code from the tag is input into a computer. The computer carries out a check on the code.

Describe **one** check which may be carried out on the code.

_____

_____

1
0

(iii) Give **one** advantage to the shop of using this input method.

_____

_____

1
0

(d) Jagheer uses _electronic funds transfer at point of sale_ (EFTPOS) to pay for the dungarees.

    (i) Give **one** advantage to Jagheer of using EFTPOS.

_____

_____

1
0

    (ii) Give **one** advantage to the shop of using EFTPOS.

_____

_____

1
0

(e) Some information about the dungarees is processed using _interactive processing_.

What is meant by interactive processing?

_____

_____

1
0

(f) The shop uses _batch processing_ to process information about its employees' pay.

What is meant by batch processing?

_____

_____

1
0

7.

NEW OPERATING SYSTEM
VERSION 5.2
Includes:
CD ROM DRIVE
FLOPPY DISC DRIVE
540 Mb HARD DISC DRIVE
MOUSE
KEYBOARD
PRINTER
and
BASIC

(a) The computer shown in the advert can use a CD ROM, a floppy disc and a hard disc.

   (i) Describe a situation where a CD ROM would be used rather than a hard disc.

   (ii) Describe a situation where a hard disc would be used rather than a CD ROM.

(b) Describe **two** functions of the operating system of a computer.

1 _____

_____

2 _____

_____

KU | PS

1
0

1
0

2
1
0

	KU	PS

(c) BASIC is an example of a high level language. Machine code is an example of a low level language.

Describe **two** differences between a high level language and machine code.

1 _____

_____

2 _____

_____

2
1
0

(d) The printer attached to the computer uses a British *character set*.

What is meant by the term character set?

_____

_____

1
0

(e) A school science department hopes to be able to use the computer in the advert to monitor the temperature in an experiment.

The computer must use a *real time* system when it monitors the temperature.

(i) What is meant by a real time system?

_____

_____

1
0

(ii) Describe another situation where a real time system should be used.

_____

_____

1
0

[END OF QUESTION PAPER]

COMPUTING STUDIES
STANDARD GRADE
General Level

Read each question carefully.

Attempt **all** questions.

Write your answers in the space provided on the question paper.

Write as neatly as possible.

Answer in sentences wherever possible.

Before leaving the examination room you must give this book to the invigilator. If you do not, you may lose all the marks for this paper.

	KU	PS

1. John is using an integrated package to produce his Biology report. The report must include charts, graphics and text.

(a) The menu of the integrated package offers the following

       Word Processing
       Graphics
       Spreadsheet
       Database
       Communications.

  (i) Which section of the integrated package should John select to enter the text of his report?

_____

                                                                        1 / 0

  (ii) Which section of the integrated package should John select to produce simple charts?

_____

                                                                         1 / 0

(b) John reads his report and discovers that he has typed "toad" instead of "frog" throughout the report.

Describe how John could use the software to find and correct this mistake quickly and easily.

_____

_____

                                                                        1 / 0

(c) John has used a *spelling check* facility on his report.

Describe **two** limitations of a spelling check facility.

1 _____

_____

2 _____

_____   2 / 1 / 0

	KU	PS

(d) John has a photograph of a frog which he would like to include in his report.

(i) Name an input device which John could use to add the photograph as a graphic to his report.

_____

1
0

(ii) Give **one** advantage of adding the photograph as a graphic rather than sticking the photograph onto the report.

_____

_____

1
0

(e) John uses the graphics section of the integrated package to produce a drawing of a tadpole. He discovers that the drawing is too large.

What feature of the graphics package could John use to reduce the size of the drawing?

_____

_____

1
0

(f) John saves his report onto a disc and then makes a backup copy of this disc.

Give **two** reasons why John should make a backup copy.

1 _____

_____

2 _____

_____

2
1
0

2. Kiran works in the office of a small mail order company.

Details of customer accounts are kept on a computer using a database package.

Here is the information held about one of the customers.

Customer Number	:	101
Surname	:	Singh
Initial	:	J
Amount Owed	:	£50·00
Last Order	:	10th March 1998

(a) Describe how Kiran could use the database package to obtain a list of all customers in alphabetical order.

_____

_____

_____

(b) The Company wishes to offer a special discount to customers who have placed an order since 1st January 1998 and who owe less than £100.

Describe how Kiran could use the database package to obtain a list of all customers eligible for this offer.

_____

_____

_____

KU | PS

2
1
0

4
3
2
1
0

	KU	PS

(c) When Kiran starts up the database program, she types in a *password* which does not appear on the screen.

(i) Why does this password not appear on the screen?

_____

_____

1
0

(ii) Why are passwords necessary?

_____

_____

_____

2
1
0

(d) The Company used to keep the information about customers on record cards.

(i) Give **two** advantages of using a database package instead of record cards.

1 _____

_____

2 _____

_____

2
1
0

(ii) Describe **two** initial costs to the Company of setting up the computer system.

1 _____

_____

2 _____

_____

2
1
0

(iii) Describe **one** running cost to the Company of the computer system.

_____

_____

1
0

KU PS

3. Miss Lamb operates a small business that makes woollen items of clothing.

She has created the spreadsheet below to help her calculate the cost of making each item.

	A	B	C	D	E	F
1	Item	Cost of Wool	Pay per hour	Time Taken	Total Pay	Total Cost
2		(£)	(£)	(hours)	(£)	(£)
3	Sweater	8·00	3·00	3	9·00	17
4	Gloves	2·50	3·00	2	6·00	8·5
5	Scarf	5·00	2·50	1	2·50	7·5
6	Hat	3·00	2·75	1	2·75	5·75
7						

(a) Cells E3 and F3 each contain a formula.

(i) Suggest a suitable formula for cell E3.

_____

1
0

(ii) Suggest a suitable formula for cell F3.

_____

1
0

(b) The formula in E3 has been *replicated* down the other cells in column E.

(i) Explain fully the term replicate.

_____

_____

_____

2
1
0

(ii) Where else in the spreadsheet above could the replicate feature have been used?

_____

_____

2
1
0

	KU	PS

(c) Miss Lamb would like to display the contents of cell F3 as £17·00.

What must she do to the cell attributes to change the way the data appears?

_____

_____

1
0

(d) Miss Lamb would like to use a more advanced feature of the spreadsheet package. She uses the *on-line help* to assist her.

What is meant by on-line help?

_____

_____

_____

1
0

(e) Miss Lamb's friend would like to use the spreadsheet package but is unfamiliar with it. Miss Lamb recommends that he should make use of the *on-line tutorial*.

What is meant by on-line tutorial?

_____

_____

_____

1
0

	KU	PS

4. Hon San uses a bank which operates TelBank, a telephone banking service.

(a) When Hon San makes use of TelBank he is asked for his name and *Personal Identification Number (PIN)*.

Why is a Personal Identification Number (PIN) necessary?

_____

_____

_____   **1 0**

(b) Hon San requests that £50 be transferred from his Cheque Account to his Savings Account.

The TelBank operator uses a computer terminal and confirms to Hon San that his instruction has been processed. The operator gives Hon San an up-to-date balance of his account.

This is an example of *interactive processing*.

(i) Explain what is meant by interactive processing.

_____

_____

_____   **1 0**

(ii) Why is interactive processing used here?

_____

_____

_____   **1 0**

	KU	PS

(c) Hon San pays a cheque into his bank account. Cheques are *batch processed* by the bank overnight.

   (i) Explain what is meant by batch processing.

      _____

      _____

      _____

   (KU: 2 1 0)

   (ii) Give **one** advantage to the bank of doing this task overnight.

      _____

      _____

   (PS: 1 0)

(d) Hon San uses a bank card to pay directly for goods in shops using *Electronic Funds Transfer (EFT)*.

   (i) Give **two** advantages to Hon San of using Electronic Funds Transfer.

     1 _____

     2 _____

   (PS: 2 1 0)

   (ii) Give **two** advantages to shops of using Electronic Funds Transfer.

     1 _____

     2 _____

   (PS: 2 1 0)

	KU	PS

5. Robonurse is a new mobile robot being introduced to work in hospitals. Its main job is to carry medicines and medical files within the hospital.

(a) When Robonurse is instructed to go from Ward 5 to Ward 10 it does so by taking the shortest route.

Explain how Robonurse finds the correct route to take.

_____

_____

1
0

(b) When Robonurse moves around the hospital it is able to avoid bumping into people and other objects.

Explain clearly how Robonurse is able to do this.

_____

_____

_____

2
1
0

(c) Robonurse works in *real-time*.

What is meant by the term real-time?

_____

_____

1
0

	KU	PS

(d) The medicines and medical files used to be carried by the nurses.

    (i) Give **one advantage** for the nurses of having this job done by Robonurse.

       _____

       _____   1 0

    (ii) Give **one disadvantage** for the nurses of having this job done by Robonurse.

       _____

       _____   1 0

(e) Describe **two disadvantages** for the hospital management of buying and using Robonurse.

    1 _____

       _____

    2 _____   2 1 0

       _____

(f) The computer built into Robonurse is a *dedicated system*.

What is meant by the term dedicated system?

_____

_____   1 0

KU | PS

6. Here is an advertisement from an employment magazine.

A New Job in Computing!

Programmers with High Level Language experience required to develop a new *operating system* for the 21st Century.

Must be familiar with *Graphical User Interfaces* and the very latest *voice recognition* and *handwriting recognition* techniques.

(*a*) Describe **two** functions of an operating system.

1 _____

_____

2 _____

_____

2
1
0

(*b*) What is a Graphical User Interface?

_____

_____

1
0

(*c*) Give **one** advantage of using a Graphical User Interface.

_____

_____

_____

1
0

	KU	PS

(d) BASIC, COMAL and PASCAL are examples of high level languages.

Give **two** features which are common to all high level languages.

1 _____

_____

2 _____

_____

2
1
0

(e) (i) Describe a situation where voice recognition would be useful.

_____

_____

1
0

(ii) Explain why it would be useful in this situation.

_____

_____

_____

1
0

(f) (i) Describe a situation where handwriting recognition would be useful.

_____

_____

1
0

(ii) Explain why it would be useful in this situation.

_____

_____

_____

1
0

	KU	PS

7. Sam works as a salesman. His job involves taking orders from stores all over the country.

Sam used to write the orders on paper and then enter them into a computer on his return to the office.

(a) Sam's employers have given him a laptop computer to help him collect his orders.

Why might Sam find this type of computer particularly useful?

_____

_____

PS: **1** **0**

(b) Sam has also been given a mobile phone.

What additional device does he need to send his orders from his laptop to his office computer?

_____

KU: **1** **0**

(c) The computers in Sam's office are connected in a Local Area Network (LAN).

Describe **two** advantages of having the computers linked in this way.

1 _____

_____

2 _____

_____

KU: **2** **1** **0**

KU	PS

(*d*) Sam does not need to visit his office as often as before.

   (i) Give **one** advantage this may have for Sam.

_____

_____

_____

| | 1 0 |

   (ii) Give **one** advantage this may have for Sam's employers.

_____

_____

_____

| | 1 0 |

(*e*) Sam's laptop computer has a CD ROM drive.

Give **one** advantage of using a CD ROM rather than a floppy disc.

_____

_____

_____

| 1 0 | |

(*f*) The laptop computer has a *Liquid Crystal Display (LCD)*.

Give **one** reason why a laptop computer has a Liquid Crystal Display (LCD).

_____

_____

| 1 0 | |

[*END OF QUESTION PAPER*]

1999
MONDAY, 24 MAY
G/C   9.00 AM – 10.15 AM
F/**G** 10.20 AM – 11.35 AM

COMPUTING STUDIES
STANDARD GRADE
General Level

Read each question carefully.

Attempt **all** questions.

Write your answers in the space provided on the question paper.

Write as neatly as possible.

Answer in sentences wherever possible.

Before leaving the examination room you must give this book to the invigilator. If you do not, you may lose all the marks for this paper.

	KU	PS

1. Clark is a news reporter working for the Daily Globe.

   (a) He has a palmtop computer which uses handwriting recognition to help him to take notes.

   Why might Clark find this type of computer particularly useful?

   _____

   _____

   _____

   _____

   1
   0 (PS)

   (b) When Clark returns to his office he is able to transfer his notes onto his desktop computer.

   He uses a wordprocessing package to edit his story.

   State **two** features of the wordprocessing package that Clark might find useful.

   1 _____

   _____

   2 _____

   _____

   2
   1
   0 (KU)

   (c) Clark is unfamiliar with a particular feature of the software. He is able to make use of the *on-line help* facility.

   What is meant by on-line help?

   _____

   _____

   _____

   _____

   1
   0 (KU)

	KU	PS

(d) The desktop computers in Clark's office are linked together in a *local area network*.

Give **two** advantages of having computers linked in this type of network.

1 _____

_____

2 _____

_____

2
1
0

(e) The *command-driven* software package being used is to be replaced by a *menu-driven* package.

Describe **one** advantage of a menu-driven package over a command-driven package.

_____

_____

_____

_____

1
0

(f) The new package is to have a *Graphical User Interface*.

What is a Graphical User Interface?

_____

_____

_____

1
0

KU	PS

2. A college uses a computerised database package to hold information about its students.

Here is part of the information held about one of the students.

Student Reference Number	:	980123
Name	:	Kearney, Jane
Class	:	S1MZ
Course	:	Chemistry
Gender	:	Female

(a) The college wishes to have a list of all students in alphabetical order.

Describe how you could use the database to list all students in alphabetical order.

_____

_____

_____

_____

2
1
0

(b) (i) The college wishes to send a letter to all female students studying Computer Science.

On which **two fields** do they need to search?

Field 1 _____

Field 2 _____

2
1
0

(ii) As well as the database package, what other package will be required in order to carry out this mail shot?

_____

1
0

	KU	PS

(c) The database stores confidential information.

Describe **two** ways of ensuring there is no unauthorised access to the database.

1 _____

_____

2 _____

_____

PS: **2 1 0**

(d) The college is worried that the information in the database could be accidentally lost.

Describe a precaution that could be taken to avoid this happening.

_____

_____

KU: **1 0**

(e) Jane would like to see all the information held about her on the computer database.

Is she entitled to see this information? _____

Explain your answer. _____

_____

_____

KU: **2 1 0**

3. A company rents out houses and flats. It uses a spreadsheet to keep a record of its income and expenditure.

Here is part of the spreadsheet.

	A	B	C	D	E
1	Property	January	February	March	Quarterly Total
2					
3	Aberdeen				
4	income	250	250	300	800
5	expenditure	15	15	20	50
6	Dundee				
7	income	130	130	150	410
8	expenditure	25	25	27	77
9	Edinburgh				
10	income	300	300	350	950
11	expenditure	30	30	45	105
12	Glasgow				
13	income	295	295	250	840
14	expenditure	35	35	30	100
15					
16	Monthly Income	975	975	1050	
17					
18	Monthly Expenditure	105	105	122	
19					
20					

(a) Cells E4 and B16 each contain a formula.

(i) Suggest a suitable formula for cell E4.

_____

(ii) Suggest a suitable formula for cell B16.

_____

	KU	PS

(b) The formula in B16 has been *replicated* across to the other cells in row 16.

   (i) What is meant by the term replicate in this example?

        _____

        _____

        _____

KU: 2 1 0

   (ii) Where else in the spreadsheet could the replicate feature have been used?

        _____

        _____

        _____

PS: 2 1 0

(c) The company buys some property in Inverness and wishes to include this in the spreadsheet.

Describe how this can be done.

    _____

    _____

    _____

    _____

PS: 2 1 0

(d) The company wishes to produce a quarterly report showing data from the spreadsheet in a graph.

What feature of the spreadsheet package could be used to do this?

    _____

    _____

KU: 1 0

	KU	PS

4. John does his shopping in a supermarket.

The supermarket provides him with a hand-held scanner so that he can scan his purchases.

> ### Scan
> ### *as you go* . . .
>
> With new Handiscan you scan goods as you go to show what you have spent and exactly how many items you have.

(*a*) (i) What part of the packaging does John scan?

_____

1
0

(ii) Give **three** pieces of information which can be obtained from the scanned code.

1 _____

2 _____

3 _____

3
2
1
0

(iii) A computer carries out a check on the scanned code.

Give **one** check which may be carried out on the code.

_____

_____

1
0

(iv) Give **one** advantage to John of using this hand-held scanner.

_____

_____

1
0

(v) The scanner has a *Liquid Crystal Display (LCD)*.
State **one** advantage of an LCD display.

_____

1
0

	KU	PS

(b) John has a bank card which he can use to obtain cash from the in-store Automated Telling Machine (cash dispenser).

   (i) Describe **two** other types of transactions that John could make using the Automated Telling Machine.

_____

_____

_____   **2 1 0**

_____

  (ii) When John uses his bank card to obtain cash, he enters a code.

Explain why he is asked to enter this code.

_____

_____   **1 0**

(c) John decides to pay for his shopping by cheque.

  (i) What name is given to the special characters printed on cheques which allow them to be processed very quickly?

_____   **1 0**

  (ii) Describe **two** disadvantages to the supermarket in accepting a cheque.

1 _____

_____

2 _____   **2 1 0**

_____

(d) Banks use *batch processing* to process cheques.

What is meant by batch processing?

_____

_____   **1 0**

	KU	PS

5. (*a*) OS/2, UNIX, Windows 98 and Macintosh OS8 are some examples of *operating system* programs.

State **two** tasks an operating system would carry out.

1 _____

_____

2 _____

2
1
0

_____

(*b*) BASIC, COMAL and PASCAL are examples of *high level programming languages*.

Describe **two** features common to high level languages.

1 _____

_____

2 _____

2
1
0

_____

(*c*) (i) A program is entered into a computer using a keyboard.

Is the program stored in RAM or ROM?

_____

1
0

(ii) The program uses a data file.

Explain the difference between a program and a data file.

_____

2
1
0

_____

	KU	PS

(*d*) A computer has a *main memory size* of 8 megabytes. It has an *operating system* which occupies 2 megabytes.

   (i) Will a program which requires 7 megabytes of main memory run on this computer?

   _____

   Give a reason for your answer.

   _____

   _____

   2
   1
   0

   (ii) The owner adds more memory to the computer.

   Give **two** reasons why she might have done this.

   1 _____

   _____

   2 _____

   _____

   2
   1
   0

(*e*) Give **one** advantage and **one** disadvantage of having software supplied on ROM.

   Advantage _____

   _____

   Disadvantage _____

   _____

   2
   1
   0

	KU	PS

6. A space shuttle craft carries a robotic arm to assist with repairs to a space station. The robotic arm is fitted to the outside of the shuttle craft.

(a) Give **two** reasons why a robotic arm is used in this situation.

1 _____

_____

2 _____

_____

PS: 2 1 0

(b) A computer inside the shuttle is used to control the robotic arm. The computer uses *closed loop* control.

Explain what is meant by closed loop control.

_____

_____

_____

KU: 2 1 0

(c) The robotic arm was designed using a professional Computer Aided Design (CAD) package.

(i) Give **two** advantages of using a CAD package to draw the plans rather than drawing them by hand.

1 _____

_____

2 _____

_____

KU: 2 1 0

(ii) A professional CAD system has a mouse and a printer.

Give **one** other input and **one** other output device you would expect it to have.

INPUT DEVICE: _____

OUTPUT DEVICE: _____

KU: 2 1 0

	KU	PS

7. Kulvinder wishes to use his home computer to connect to the Internet. This means he wants to link his computer to other computers all over the world.

   (a) What additional hardware and software will Kulvinder require for his computer?

   Hardware: _____

   Software: _____

   PS: 2 1 0

   (b) What type of network will Kulvinder's computer be linked to?

   _____

   KU: 1 0

   (c) Give **two** advantages of being connected to the Internet.

   1 _____

   _____

   2 _____

   _____

   PS: 2 1 0

   (d) Kulvinder is able to work from home using his computer.

   (i) Give **two** advantages for Kulvinder of being able to work from home.

   1 _____

   _____

   2 _____

   _____

   PS: 2 1 0

   (ii) Why might Kulvinder dislike working from home?

   _____

   _____

   PS: 1 0

[END OF QUESTION PAPER]

NATIONAL QUALIFICATIONS 2000

FRIDAY, 9 JUNE
G/C 1.00 PM–2.15 PM
F/G 2.20 PM–3.35 PM

COMPUTING STUDIES
STANDARD GRADE
General Level

Read each question carefully.

Attempt **all** questions.

Write your answers in the space provided on the question paper.

Write as neatly as possible.

Answer in sentences wherever possible.

Before leaving the examination room you must give this book to the invigilator. If you do not, you may lose all the marks for this paper.

	KU	PS

1. (*a*) Moira works as a lawyer. She has to write many letters that contain the same legal paragraphs.

   How could she use a word processing package to make this job easier?

   _____

   PS: 1 0

   (*b*) One of the documents that Moira has typed is 15 pages long. Having just finished it she realises that she has included the phrase "The Scottish Office" 74 times when she should have typed "The Scottish Parliament".

   Explain how she could use her word processing package to correct this error.

   _____

   _____

   _____

   PS: 3 2 1 0

   (*c*) Moira's computer system has a standard character set.

   What does a character set contain?

   _____

   _____

   _____

   KU: 3 2 1 0

	KU	PS

(*d*) Moira always tries to be sure that there are no spelling mistakes in her documents.

What feature of the word processing package helps Moira do this?

_____

1
0

(*e*) Sometimes when documents are examined for spelling errors the word processor highlights a correctly spelled word.

Give **one** example of a word that would be highlighted even though correctly spelled.

_____

1
0

(*f*) Moira notices a spelling mistake in the letter that the word processor hasn't highlighted.

Give **one** example of an error that may not be detected by the word processor.

_____

1
0

(*g*) When she visits clients Moira makes notes of their discussion on a *palmtop computer*.

What feature must the palmtop computer have to allow Moira to write her notes directly onto the palmtop?

_____

1
0

(*h*) Moira had thought about using a *laptop computer* instead of a palmtop.

Why did Moira decide to use a palmtop rather than a laptop?

_____

1
0

2. Nasar's guitar shop uses a computerised database to keep track of stock.

An example of a record from the database is shown below.

```
Record 431

Guitar   : Electric
Model    : FS101
In Stock : 10
Colour   : Blue
Cost     : £250
```

(a) Angie wishes to buy an electric guitar for less than £300.

(i) How could the shop assistant use the database to see if any suitable guitars are available?

_____

_____

_____

_____

(ii) How does the shop assistant know if that particular guitar is available?

_____

3
2
1
0

1
0

(b) (i) The shop assistant wishes to see a list of suitable stock on her monitor. She changes the display of records from **Display 1** to **Display 2**, as shown below.

```
                    Record 431

        Guitar   :  Electric
        Model    :  FS101
        In Stock :  10
        Colour   :  Blue
        Cost     :  £250
```

Display 1

Guitar	Model	In Stock	Colour	Cost
Electric	FS101	10	Blue	£250
Electric	AX21	4	Brown	£150

Display 2

What has the shop assistant done so that the stock information appears like Display 2?

_____

_____

(ii) The shop assistant uses the database to produce a *hard copy* of stock.

What is hard copy?

_____

(c) Nasar's computerised database system makes use of a *program* and a *data* file.

(i) What is a program?

_____

_____

(ii) What is a data file?

_____

_____

KU	PS

1 0

1 0

1 0

1 0

65

3. David has been asked to write a computer program for the local library.

(a) David is familiar with high level languages and low level languages.

Identify **two** common features of high level languages that might persuade David to write the program using a high level language rather than using a low level language.

_____

_____

_____

_____

2
1
0

(b) What is David's program translated into for the computer to understand it?

_____

1
0

(c) The librarian would like to insert a photograph at the top of all letters sent out from the library.

What input device could David use to transfer the photograph to the library computer?

_____

1
0

4. Fly Electronic manufactures flight simulators. Mobile robots take parts from the stockroom to the area of the factory where the flight simulators are assembled.

(*a*) When it was decided to change from a manual stockroom to an automated stockroom, the managers had to consider certain costs.

(i) Suggest **two** costs that the managers had to consider when introducing the new system.

1 _____

_____

2 _____

_____

(ii) Suggest **one** way that savings have been made since the introduction of the automated system.

_____

_____

(*b*) The mobile robots follow white lines as they travel to the factory assembly area.

(i) Explain how a mobile robot could follow a white line.

_____

_____

_____

_____

_____

KU	PS
2 1 0	
1 0	
3 2 1 0	

KU	PS

(ii) Suggest **two** safety precautions the factory owners should take in the areas where the mobile robots travel.

1 _____

_____

2 _____

_____

2
1
0

(c) Suggest **one** reason why airlines would spend money on a flight simulator to train pilots before allowing them to fly a real aircraft.

_____

_____

1
0

(d) The flight simulators built by Fly Electronic use a *real time* operating system.

Why do they use a real time operating system?

_____

_____

1
0

	KU	PS

5. Graphic Services provide artwork for advertisements.

Hamaira has just started to work for Graphic Services and has been asked to use a graphics package to prepare a logo for Arrow Computers.

(*a*) (i) Graphic Services decided against choosing a graphics package with a *command driven* Human Computer Interface (*HCI*).

Why do you think they didn't like a command driven interface?

_____

_____

> PS 1 0

(ii) Graphic Services decided that they would prefer their computers to operate a *WIMP* style Human Computer Interface (HCI). WIMP is an example of a type of user interface.

What **type** of user interface is WIMP an example of?

_____

> KU 1 0

(*b*) (i) Before she started work on the logo for Arrow Computers, Hamaira used an *on-line tutorial* of the graphics package.

What is an on-line tutorial?

_____

_____

> KU 1 0

(ii) Hamaira used the *on-line help* facility of the graphics package while working on the logo.

What is on-line help?

_____

_____

> KU 1 0

KU	PS

(c) When Hamaira created a logo she started with **Logo A** below. Eventually she changed it to **Logo B** below.

Logo A   **Logo B**

What features of the graphics package did Hamaira use in changing from **Logo A** to **Logo B**?

_____

_____

(d) When her designs are finished, Hamaira sends them to her boss, who works in the same building. The company have their computers linked using a network.

What type of network does Graphic Services use so that Hamaira can send her work to her boss?

_____

(e) The heading of letters sent out by Graphic Services used to look like **Letter X** below.

Letter X

> Graphic Services
> Excellence in Design
> 01555 314157

The heading was recently changed to look like **Letter Y** below.

Letter Y

> Graphic Services
> Excellence in Design
> 01555 314157

How would Graphic Services change the heading from **Letter X** to look like **Letter Y**?

_____

_____

2
1
0

1
0

1
0

2000

	KU	PS

(f) Graphic Services used to have all their work drawn by hand. There were no computers.

Suggest **two** changes to the working conditions of the employees of Graphic Services as a result of the introduction of computers.

1 _____

_____

2 _____

_____

2
1
0

(g) State **one** precaution Graphic Services could take to ensure that no unauthorised person gains access to their data.

_____

_____

1
0

(h) Hamaira is allowed access to the data held about her by Graphic Services.

(i) Give **one** example of an organisation that may have information on Hamaira which she would **not** have the right to see.

_____

1
0

(ii) Why are individuals not allowed to see such data?

_____

_____

1
0

71

6. Ka Lai Ho has created a spreadsheet to show all stock items sold by Video Tape Retailers. Part of the spreadsheet is shown below.

	A	B	C	D	E
1	Video Title	Category	Cost	Number Sold	Total Sales
2	Catch that Rat	Cartoon	£9·99	51	£509
3	Football Bloopers	Comedy	£11·49	8	£92
4	Greatest Stunts	Action	£11·49	3	£34
5	Heroines	Romantic	£14·50	23	£334

(a) Ka Lai entered the formula =C2*D2 in cell E2 to calculate the Total Sales. Similar formulae are required in cells E3 to E5.

What feature of a spreadsheet package could be used for this?

(b) The data appears in the spreadsheet in alphabetical order of Video Title.

(i) Ka Lai wants to place more data into the spreadsheet.

How can she enter the following data in its correct place?

Video Title	:	Have you gone crazy?
Category	:	Comedy
Cost	:	£13.99
Number sold	:	20

(ii) The video title "**Have you gone crazy?**" will be too long for its cell.

How can Ka Lai make sure that the whole of the title will be seen in its cell?

(c) Column E shows the total money the shop takes for each video title. Ka Lai would like to show the amount in pounds and pence.

What should she do so that the value £34 in E4 appears correctly as £34·47?

7. (a) Petrol King has 125 petrol stations around Scotland. They recently introduced computer systems into each petrol station. They made use of a *systems analyst* and a computer *engineer*.

PETROL KING

(i) What does a systems analyst do?

_____

_____

_____

1
0

(ii) What does a computer engineer do?

_____

_____

_____

1
0

(b) Petrol King's customers can pay for petrol using EFT.

(i) What does EFT stand for?

E _____ F _____ T _____

1
0

(ii) Describe **one** benefit to Petrol King when customers pay by EFT.

_____

_____

_____

1
0

(iii) Describe **one** benefit to the customers in paying by EFT.

_____

_____

1
0

(c) All 125 petrol station computers are linked to the mainframe computer at Petrol King's headquarters. At the end of each week the sales figures are sent to the mainframe computer.

What **type** of network is needed to connect all of the computers together?

_____

(d) Chris runs a Petrol King petrol station. He would like to keep a good quality printout of his weekly sales figures.

Would he be better to buy an *ink jet* or a *dot matrix* printer? Explain your answer.

_____

_____

_____

(e) Chris wants to calculate the amount of sales made of petrol and diesel, and use the information to produce a chart of these values every month. Select **one** package from the list below that could let him perform both functions.

Word Processor ☐

Graphics ☐

Spreadsheet ☐

Communications ☐

(f) At home Chris has his own personal computer. He saw an advertisement for a newer *operating system* than the one he uses just now.

Identify **two** different tasks that an operating system carries out.

_____

_____

KU	PS
	1
	0
	2
	1
	0
	1
	0
2	
1	
0	

8. The Bank of Scotia has many cash machines connected from around the country to its mainframe in Edinburgh. This allows customers easy access to their money.

(a) The bank uses an *interactive* operating system.

Why should it use an interactive operating system for this type of work?

_____

_____

_____

(b) The Bank of Scotia wishes to improve the cash machine service by providing *voice output* for customers.

Describe **one** disadvantage to customers of this system.

_____

_____

_____

(c) Suggest **one** reason why the use of *voice recognition* at the cash machines may not work well.

_____

_____

_____

KU	PS
	1
	0
	1
	0
	1
	0

(d) The bank uses *MICR* to process cheques.

    (i) What does MICR stand for?

    M ——————— I ——————— C ——————— R ———————

    (ii) State **two** benefits to the bank of using MICR.

(e) The Bank of Scotia has recently replaced the terminals used inside the bank. The new terminals have *LCD* screens.

What do the letters LCD stand for?

    L ——————— C ——————— D ———————

(f) Each day the Bank of Scotia processes thousands of items of *data*. Staff in the bank describe this as processing *information*.

Explain the terms data and information.

[END OF QUESTION PAPER]

KU	PS
1 0	
	2 1 0
1 0	
2 1 0	

1996
MONDAY, 20 MAY
1.30 PM – 3.15 PM

COMPUTING STUDIES
STANDARD GRADE
Credit Level

Read each question carefully.

Attempt **all** questions.

Write your answers in the answer book provided. **Do not** write on the question paper.

Write as neatly as possible.

Answer in sentences wherever possible.

1. A school uses a computer system to help pupils choose a career. Each pupil completes a *mark sense card*, as shown in the diagram below, to record subjects taken and other details. The cards are processed by the computer department in a local college using a mainframe computer.

KU	PS

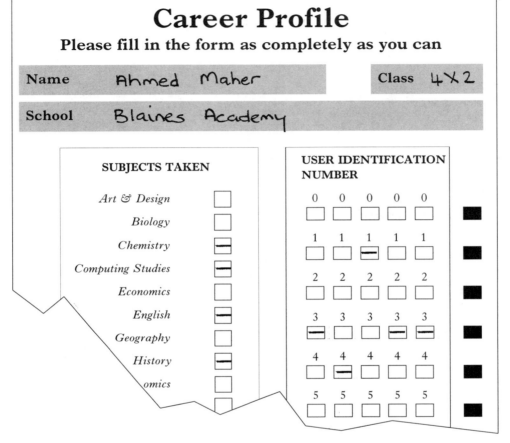

(a) (i) How will the data on the mark sense card be input to the computer system?   **1**

    (ii) Give **two** advantages to the college of using mark sense cards for data input.   **2**

(b) Each pupil has a 5-digit user identification number. The last digit is a *check digit*.

    (i) Why must the pupil's identification number be entered on the card?   **1**

    (ii) What is the purpose of the check digit in the user identification number?   **2**

(c) The cards are *batch processed*. Give **two** advantages to the college of using batch processing.   **2**

(d) Each pupil's name, school, date of birth and user identification number has already been entered into the computer. These details are held on a pupil master file. The date of birth was entered as three separate numeric fields—year, month, day. Describe how the **month** field could have been validated.   **2**

(e) The data from each pupil's Career Profile card is held on a transactions file. The pupil master file and the transactions file are held on magnetic tape. What must be done to the transactions file before processing can begin?   **2**

| | KU | PS |

2. Walter works for a local hospital radio service called Radio Royal. He suggests that the catalogue of music CDs should be computerised. He buys an integrated package which has a *graphical user interface* and *static data linkage*.

(*a*) What is meant by

    (i) graphical user interface   **2**

    (ii) static data linkage?   **2**

(*b*) Walter decides to use the database section of the package to store the information about the music CDs. Each track on a CD will have Track Number, Title, Artist and Playing Time, as shown below.

Radio Royal
HOSPITAL BROADCASTING

CD INPUT DOCUMENT

Track Number	Title	Artist	Playing Time (mins)
458	Boo!	Michael and the Bandits	3.28
462	Away with you	Ket and Beth	4.02

    (i) Suggest a suitable length for each of the fields. Calculate the number of bytes required to store 1 record. **Show all working.**   **3**

    (ii) There are 2000 music tracks in the library. Approximately how many kilobytes will be required to store the entire file? **Show all working.**   **2**

(*c*) Walter wants a list of tracks by **Michael and the Bandits**. Each track must be less than 4 minutes. He wants the tracks listed in order of Track Number. Describe how Walter could use the database section of the package to produce this list.   **3**

(*d*) Radio Royal relies on donations from many people. Walter wants to store details about these people. He knows that there are certain legal requirements about holding personal data on computer. What must he do to meet these legal requirements **before** holding personal data on computer?   **2**

(*e*) Radio Royal would like to send standard letters to the people who give donations. Outline the steps involved in producing a *standard letter*.   **3**

	KU	PS

3. (*a*) High level languages need to be translated. A program written in a high level language can be *compiled* or *interpreted*. Give **two** advantages that a compiled program has over an interpreted program.

    2

(*b*) Software written in a high level language is said to be portable. What is meant by *portability of software*?

    1

(*c*) An operating system is a program which controls the operation of a computer. Some operating systems allow *multi-access*.

  (i) What is meant by multi-access?

    1

  (ii) Describe a situation where multi-access would be useful.

    2 (PS)

(*d*) One of the functions of the Operating System is file management. The diagram below shows how a user organises her files.

  (i) What type of filing system has she used?

    1

  (ii) Describe **two** benefits of using this type of filing system. Use examples from the diagram above to illustrate your answer.

    2 (PS)

(*e*) Programs often require calculations to be carried out. Which part of the Central Processing Unit (CPU) performs calculations?

    1

(*f*) A number such as $832{\cdot}471$ can be represented as $0{\cdot}832471 \times 10^3$. Explain how this might be represented in *floating-point*. (The numbers are actually stored in binary, but use decimal in your explanation.)

    2

(*g*) Text can be represented by using a code for each character. ASCII code is a standard code for representing characters.

  (i) Give **one** advantage of representing characters using a standard code such as ASCII.

    1

  (ii) Some of the ASCII codes represent *control characters*. Give **two** examples of uses for control characters.

    2

	KU	PS

4. (*a*) A section of road is being resurfaced. Temporary traffic lights are being used to control the traffic. Drivers are stopped at the traffic lights, as shown below. They can see there are no cars coming the other way, but they still have to wait a long time for the lights to change.

  (i) In this situation, is it more likely that the traffic lights are controlled by an open or a closed loop system? Give a reason for your answer. — PS **1**

  (ii) Describe how the use of sensors could improve the traffic flow. — PS **2**

  (iii) Suggest a suitable type of sensor for this situation. — PS **1**

(*b*) (i) A company is thinking of introducing robot arms to parts of its factory. Explain why a *systems analysis* needs to be carried out before the robot arms are introduced. — KU **2**

  (ii) The company buys robot arms which have six *degrees of freedom*. What is meant by degrees of freedom? — KU **1**

  (iii) Each robot arm has an analogue pressure sensor fitted. Why is it necessary for the computer which controls the robots to have an analogue to digital converter? — KU **1**

(*c*) The control software for a robot can be held either on disc or in ROM.

  (i) Give **one** advantage of disc-based software. — KU **1**

  (ii) Give **one** advantage of ROM-based software. — KU **1**

		KU	PS

5. (*a*) A college uses a computer system to help with the designs of fabrics and clothes. It uses a *spreadsheet* to calculate costs. Part of the spreadsheet is shown below.

	A	B	C	D	E
1	CALCULATION OF TOTAL COST				
2					
3	Material	Unit	Cost per unit	Units used	Total
4			£		£
5	Cotton	metres	7·28	1	7·28
6	Stiffening	metres	3·65	2	7·30
7	Thread	reels	0·58	3	1·74
8	Zip fasteners	each	0·92	2	1·84

(i) When the spreadsheet was set up, a formula was put in cell E5. Suggest a suitable formula. **[PS 1]**

(ii) The formula in cell E5 was then copied into cells E6 to E8. Would this copying have used *relative referencing* or *absolute referencing*? Explain your answer. **[PS 2]**

(iii) Cells A3 to E3 have *cell protection* set to ON. What is meant by cell protection? **[KU 1]**

(*b*) The college is considering using *virtual reality* to model some of the designs.

(i) What is meant by virtual reality? **[KU 2]**

(ii) What additional output device might the college need to purchase for a virtual reality system? **[KU 1]**

	KU	PS

6. (*a*) The internet is a world-wide system for computer communication. Computer users can use the internet to communicate with each other and to access large databases of information.

What would you need, as well as your computer system and a telephone line, to gain access to a large network such as this? Give **two** answers.

KU: 2

(*b*) A group of primary school children is carrying out a project on the different life styles and customs of children in another country. Suggest **two** ways in which access to the internet might assist them with this project.

PS: 2

(*c*) Some databases can only be accessed by users who have proper authorisation.

　(i) Suggest **one example** of a database that might be restricted in this way.

PS: 1

　(ii) A user has been given authorisation to gain access to a restricted database. Describe **two** steps involved in gaining authorisation.

KU: 2

(*d*) Some users of wide area networks are concerned that access to other computers will make their computer systems more liable to catching a virus. A virus is a piece of code in a program which can alter data, and can cause computers to fail.

What piece of legislation has been introduced to try to restrict the spread of viruses?

KU: 2

[END OF QUESTION PAPER]

COMPUTING STUDIES
STANDARD GRADE
Credit Level

Read each question carefully.

Attempt **all** questions.

Write your answers in the answer book provided. **Do not** write on the question paper.

Write as neatly as possible.

Answer in sentences wherever possible.

	KU	PS

1. Beth has an old computer system, and considers buying some new software. She considers buying an integrated package, but thinks that her computer is probably too out-of-date to run this package.

(a) Give **two** possible explanations why her computer may not be able to run this software.

    PS: 2

(b) Beth buys separate packages instead of an integrated package. Give **two** disadvantages to Beth of buying separate packages.

    PS: 2

(c) Beth uses a word processing package to help her produce *standard letters*.

    (i) What is a standard letter?

    KU: 2

    (ii) What additional application package is she likely to use when producing standard letters?

    PS: 1

    (iii) When Beth tries to print out her letters, her printer does not print. An error message on the screen says "No Printer Driver". What is a *printer driver*, and why is it needed?

    KU: 2

(d) Beth uses a spreadsheet package to help with her accounts.

    (i) In the instruction manual of the spreadsheet, reference is made to cell B4. What is a *cell*?

    KU: 1

    (ii) After reading the manual, Beth enters data into a spreadsheet. Some cells have formulae in them, so she decides to protect these cells. What is meant by *cell protection*?

    KU: 1

KU | PS

2. There are some similarities between a database and a spreadsheet. Part of a database and part of a spreadsheet are shown below.

Database

Record 2

Name :   Molly Strachan

Test 1 :   4

Test 2 :   8

Average :   6

Spreadsheet

	A	B	C	D
1		Class 1X1A Test		
2				
3	Name	Test 1	Test 2	Average
4				
5	Alex Smith	17	13	15
6	Molly Strachan	4	8	6
7	Mike Conlon	20	16	

(*a*)   A *computed field* in a database is similar to a formula in a spreadsheet. Explain what is meant by a computed field.   **2**

(*b*)   (i)   What part of the spreadsheet shown above holds the same information as a **record** in the database?   **1**

(ii)   What part of the spreadsheet shown above holds the same information as a **field** in the database?   **1**

(*c*)   The formula (B5 + C5)/2 is in cell D5 of the spreadsheet. The formula is replicated to cell D7.

(i)   What would the **formula** be in cell D7 if the replication was

(A)   relative?   **1**

(B)   absolute?   **1**

(ii)   Which type of replication would give the correct answer of 18 in this case?   **1**

	KU	PS

3. A teacher uses a database package to keep track of her pupils' grades. The format of a record in the database is shown below.

Field Name	Sample Data	Maximum Field Size (bytes)
Pupil	S Boyd	20
Class	2G1A	4
Date of Birth	13/02/84	8
KU	3	1
PS	3	1
PA	2	1
Overall Grade	3	1

(a) (i) Given the maximum field sizes shown above, what would be the maximum number of bytes for one record?

1

(ii) A floppy disc holds 720 kilobytes. Use your answer to part (i) above to calculate how many pupil records could be held on 1 floppy disc. **Show all working**.

2

(b) A list is required of all pupils in class 2T1F who have an overall grade of 1 or 2. Describe the steps the teacher should take to produce this list.

3

(c) The teacher would like to print a list of pupils in order of merit. This list has to show all pupils of grade 1, followed by all pupils of grade 2, etc. Pupils with the same grade have to appear alphabetically by surname. A sample of what the teacher would like is shown below.

Order of Merit   **18/3/97**

Overall Grade	Pupil
1	Conlon M
1	Singh G
2	Brown A
2	Gibson S
2	Holmes R

(i) What change would she need to make to the "Pupil" field so that she could produce the list shown above?

1

(ii) Describe the steps the teacher should take to produce this order of merit.

2

	KU	PS

(*d*) The teacher would like each pupil to input his or her own data. The database package allows the teacher to change the human computer interface (HCI). She wants to make the HCI as user-friendly as possible. Suggest **two** ways in which she could do this. — PS: 2

(*e*) The teacher realises she is holding personal information about *data subjects*.

   (i) What must she do to ensure she is within the law? — KU: 1

   (ii) Who are the data subjects in this example? — PS: 1

	KU	PS

4. A Do-It-Yourself store sells a large range of goods. The checkout at the store is shown below.

Each item for sale has a bar code printed on it, as shown in the diagram above. When an item is purchased, a bar code reader at the checkout reads the bar code on the item.

(a) Give **two** pieces of information about the item which are likely to be contained in the bar code. — KU 2

(b) Information about each item is also stored in a central computer. This information is accessed using the bar code. Give **two** pieces of information about an item which are likely to be stored by the central computer, but **not** on the bar code. — KU 2

(c) The bar code contains a *check digit*.

   (i) What is the purpose of a check digit? — KU 1

   (ii) Describe briefly how a check digit works. — KU 2

(d) Every week the staff in the store carry out a stock check. The forms they use to record the stock levels are input to the computer system using optical character recognition (OCR). Why must the staff be careful with their handwriting when filling in the OCR forms? — PS 1

(e) The store is considering using palmtop computers for stock checks. Suggest **two** advantages that palmtop computers may have over using OCR forms. — PS 2

(f) In the office, data from invoices is keyed into the computer system. This data must be verified. Suggest **two** ways in which the invoice data may be verified. — PS 2

	KU	PS

5. A car factory has had its assembly line automated. Robots now carry out most of the tasks in the assembly line.

(a) Before robots were introduced, the production in the assembly line was described as *labour intensive*. What is meant by the term labour intensive? **1**

(b) What do you think would have been the effect on productivity in the factory when robots were introduced? Give a reason for your answer. **2**

(c) Each robot on the assembly line can use a range of *end-effectors*. What is an end-effector? **1**

(d) Most of the robots have their control software in ROM. Give **two** advantages of ROM-based software. **2**

(e) When the factory was being redesigned for automation, it was known that a large area of the factory would only be used by robots. Suggest **two** features of the design of this area which could have been considered in order to reduce running costs. **2**

(f) A *systems analysis* was carried out before the assembly line was automated. Explain why a systems analysis was necessary before robots were introduced in the assembly line. **2**

	KU	PS

6. (*a*) A large company uses a mainframe computer. It runs a payroll system and a stock control system. One of these systems uses sequential access to its files, while the other uses direct access.

    (i) What type of access would the payroll system use? Explain your answer.   **2** (PS)

    (ii) What type of access would the stock control system use? Explain your answer.   **2** (PS)

(*b*) The operating system of the mainframe computer supports *multi-programming*. What is meant by the term multi-programming?   **2** (KU)

7. (*a*) Sandie buys a new computer. It is described in the shop as a *multimedia* computer. Give **one** input device and **one** output device that could justify using the word "multimedia" to describe the computer.   **2** (KU)

(*b*) The computer she buys also has a built-in *assembler*.

    (i) What is the purpose of an assembler?   **2** (KU)

    (ii) Give **one** similarity between an assembler and a compiler.   **1** (KU)

(*c*) The computer has a word size of 16 bits. What is meant by the term *word*?   **2** (KU)

(*d*) Sandie buys a printer for her computer. She is told the printer will work with her computer.

    (i) The printer is a different make from her computer. Printer manufacturers cannot check that their printers will work with **every** make of computer. How can they be sure that most characters will print out correctly?   **1** (PS)

    (ii) When Sandie keys in a £ character on her computer, her printer prints a # character. Give **one** possible explanation for this.   **1** (PS)

    (iii) Some characters on the computer do not cause anything to be printed. These are *control characters*. Give **two** examples of uses for control characters.   **2** (KU)

[END OF QUESTION PAPER]

1998
FRIDAY, 22 MAY
10.30 AM – 12.15 PM

COMPUTING STUDIES
STANDARD GRADE
Credit Level

Read each question carefully.

Attempt **all** questions.

Write your answers in the answer book provided. **Do not** write on the question paper.

Write as neatly as possible.

Answer in sentences wherever possible.

	KU	PS

1. Fahrat has recently bought a new computer, and is considering buying some software for it.

    (a) She is unsure whether to buy an *integrated package*, or separate *applications packages*.

        (i) Give **two** advantages of buying an integrated package.   **KU 2**

        (ii) Give **one** disadvantage of buying an integrated package.   **KU 1**

    (b) Fahrat decides to buy an integrated package. She wants to enter data into a spreadsheet and use this data to draw a graph. She needs to change the data regularly. Should she choose an integrated package with *dynamic data linkage* or *static data linkage*? Explain your answer.   **PS 2**

    (c) She uses the integrated package to produce *standard letters* with her computer.

        (i) What is a standard letter?   **KU 2**

        (ii) Outline the main steps in producing a standard letter.   **PS 3**

    (d) The Word Processing section of the integrated package has a *spelling check* facility. After she has used the spelling check facility on her letters, Fahrat discovers two errors which were not detected.

        (i) What does a spelling check facility do?   **KU 2**

        (ii) Give **two** examples of words which could have passed the spelling check but could be wrongly spelt.   **PS 2**

    (e) Fahrat wants to print out some of her work.

        (i) What software must be available to ensure that her work prints out on paper with the same text appearance as she made on the screen?   **KU 1**

        (ii) Give **two** different styles that the software used in (e)(i) above might produce.   **PS 2**

	KU	PS

2. Christopher's parents bought a toy robotic arm for his Christmas. The robotic arm can do some simple tasks on its own, or it can be connected to his computer to carry out more complex tasks.

(*a*) The robotic arm came with three separate *end effectors*.

    (i) What is meant by the term end effector?   **KU 1**

    (ii) Suggest **one** possible end effector for this toy.   **PS 1**

(*b*) The robotic arm has 6 *degrees of freedom*.

    (i) What is meant by the term degrees of freedom?   **KU 1**

    (ii) The wrist can only move up and down. How many degrees of freedom does it have?   **PS 1**

(*c*) When the robotic arm works on its own, the control software is held in ROM. When the arm is connected to Christopher's computer, the control software can be loaded from disc.

    (i) Give **one** advantage of holding the software in ROM.   **KU 1**

    (ii) Give **one** advantage of being able to load the software from disc.   **KU 1**

(*d*) Christopher tries to make his robotic arm pick up an egg from the floor. He finds the arm breaks the egg every time.

    (i) Is it more likely that the robotic arm is controlled by an *open loop* or a *closed loop* system? Give a reason for your answer.   **PS 2**

    (ii) Describe how the use of a *sensor* could enable the eggs to be picked up without breaking them.   **PS 2**

	KU	PS

3. The internet is a world-wide network used for computer communication. A supermarket chain is considering offering goods for sale on the internet.

(a) A user has a computer system with a modem and a telephone line. What else would he need to gain access to the internet? **1**

(b) Suggest **one** kind of person for whom internet shopping would be attractive. **1**

(c) The items could be made available to the user as a **spreadsheet**. An example of the spreadsheet is shown below.

	A	B	C	D	E	F	G	H
1		**Fred Bloggs Supermarket**						
2								
3	VAT Rate:	17·5 %						
4								
5			Unit	Number	Net		Total	
6	Description	Size	Cost	Purchased	Cost	VAT	Cost	
7								
8	Corn Flakes	750 g	£2·23	2	£4·46	£0·78	£5·24	
9	Beans	25 g	£0·45	4	£1·80	£0·32	£2·12	
10	Eggs	Medium	£0·40		£0·00	£0·00	£0·00	
11								
12								

(i) The user will enter data in column D to order particular items. What can be done to the spreadsheet to prevent other cells being overwritten? **1**

(ii) When the user entered the value 2 in cell D8, the amount £4·46 appeared in cell E8. Suggest a suitable formula for cell E8. **2**

(iii) A formula is placed in cell F8 to calculate the VAT for Corn Flakes. This formula refers to cells B3 and E8. It is replicated down the column.

Would the reference to B3 use *relative referencing* or *absolute referencing*? Explain your answer. **2**

(iv) How must the supermarket alter the spreadsheet if an extra item is added to stock? **1**

	KU	PS

(d) The items could be made available to the user as a **database**.

   (i) If the spreadsheet had 2000 rows of data about products, what could you say about the size of the database?   PS: **1**

   (ii) In the spreadsheet, cell G8 was obtained as the result of a calculation. What type of field in a database would contain a calculation?   KU: **1**

   (iii) The systems analyst considered several different *Human Computer Interface (HCI)* parameters. Suggest **three** different HCI parameters that might have been considered.   KU: **3**

   (iv) How must the supermarket alter the database if an extra item is added to stock?   PS: **1**

4. (a) A computer has a *word* size of 32 bits. What is meant by the term word?   KU: **2**

(b) High level languages need to be translated. Name **two** different types of translator.   KU: **2**

(c) Some disc filing systems are *flat*, while others are *hierarchical*.

   (i) What is meant by a hierarchical filing system? Use a diagram to illustrate your answer.   KU: **2**

   (ii) Give **two** advantages that a hierarchical filing system has over a flat filing system.   KU: **2**

(d) A byte contains 8 *bits*. What is meant by the term bit?   KU: **1**

(e) The part of the computer which carries out the processing is called the *Central Processing Unit (CPU)*.

   (i) Name **two** of the main parts of the CPU.   KU: **2**

   (ii) Describe the function of **two** of the main parts of the CPU.   KU: **2**

	KU	PS

5. The Data Processing department in a steel works is designing a computerised stock control system.

(*a*) The systems analyst has to decide if the data on the stock file should be accessed *sequentially* or *randomly*. She estimates that there will be 250,000 records on the stock file. This file will be accessed approximately 18,000 times each day.

   (i) Give **one** example of a storage medium which can **only** be accessed sequentially.   **1**

   (ii) Give **one** example of a storage medium which can be accessed randomly.   **1**

   (iii) What storage medium should she use for the stock file? Give an explanation for your answer.   **2**

(*b*) The systems analyst gives a stock code to each item in the stores. The last digit in each stock code is a *check digit*.

   (i) Give **one** reason why she uses a check digit.   **1**

   (ii) Suggest **one** way in which data could be *verified*.   **1**

(*c*) When an item is removed from stock, the code number must be entered into the computer. The systems analyst decides that the processing of transactions should be carried out by *interactive processing*. Would Kimball tags, or bar codes, be more suited to interactive processing? Explain your answer.   **2**

(*d*) The systems analyst is concerned about system security, and feels that three generations of *file ancestry* should be kept.

   (i) Explain what is meant by the term file ancestry.   **1**

   (ii) Why are three generations often kept?   **2**

	KU	PS

6. A motorcyclist is in hospital following an accident.

(*a*) He could use a word processor before his accident, but can no longer use a keyboard. Suggest **one** way in which he could still input data to a word processor. ... 1

(*b*) To help his recovery, the doctors suggest that the motorcyclist tries out a *virtual reality* system.

    (i) Suggest **one** possible output device that he could use. ... 1

    (ii) Give an example of a situation in which he could use this output device. ... 1

(*c*) The internet is a world-wide network used for computer communication. The motorcyclist uses the internet to communicate with other disabled users. Give **two** reasons why voice output would be a suitable means of communication. ... 2

[END OF QUESTION PAPER]

COMPUTING STUDIES
STANDARD GRADE
Credit Level

Read each question carefully.

Attempt **all** questions.

Write your answers in the answer book provided. **Do not** write on the question paper.

Write as neatly as possible.

Answer in sentences wherever possible.

	KU	PS

1. Paula works in a large cash and carry store. Customers buy items in bulk. Sales assistants use *terminals* in the store to obtain information about stock.

   (*a*) What is a computer terminal?   **1**

   (*b*) The computer's operating system is *multi-access*.

      (i) What is meant by the term multi-access?   **2**

      (ii) Why is multi-access used here?   **1**

   (*c*) Customers feel it would be more convenient if they could order goods from their workplace computer.

   State **two** items required for remote access to the cash and carry store's computer.   **2**

   (*d*) The store keeps stock details in *master files* and *transaction files*.

   It is important that the store does not lose this data. Outline the steps involved in recovering data if

      (i) the current day's transaction file is lost   **1**

      (ii) the current day's master file is lost.   **2**

   (*e*) Paula has to perform a stock check. She writes her stock record on a form. How could the data from the form be input directly to the computer?   **1**

   (*f*) The main computer is used to produce the staff payroll. This is done using *batch processing*.

   Give **two** reasons for using batch processing.   **2**

	KU	PS

2. A finance company specialises in home improvement loans. Customer details are stored on a database. Part of a record is shown below.

Forename	Sam
Surname	Brown
Address	14 Lossie Way
Postcode	L43 6BN
Total Loan (£)	2880
Monthly payment (£)	120
Period of loan (months)	24
Number of payments to date	3
Loan paid off	No

(*a*) What is a company legally obliged to do before storing personal information on a computer?   **1**

(*b*)   (i) The finance company gives a gift voucher to all customers who have paid off a loan of £10 000 or more.

     Explain how the database is used to produce a list of such customers.   **2**

  (ii) The gift voucher is produced using *pre-printed stationery*.

     What is pre-printed stationery and why is it useful?   **2**

  (iii) Customers entitled to a gift voucher are sent a personalised *standard letter*.

     Outline the steps involved in producing this standard letter.   **3**

(*c*) Customers often telephone the finance company to enquire how much they have left to pay. Explain how you would change the record format so that the computer works out this amount.   **2**

(*d*) The company backs up its hard disc to tape.

Explain why

  (i) a hard disc is chosen for daily use   **1**

  (ii) a tape is used for backup.   **1**

(*e*) A few customers are concerned that information about themselves is held on computer.

Data subjects and *data users* are covered by legislation.

  (i) Which legislation covers storage of personal information on a computer?   **1**

  (ii) State **one** right that data subjects have under this legislation.   **1**

  (iii) State **one** responsibility that data users have under this legislation.   **1**

	KU	PS

3. Many car dealers advertise in newspapers. Details of cars for sale are kept up to date so that advertisements are accurate.

Here is a section from a typical advertisement.

Year	Make	Model	Cost(£)
1996	Vauxhall	Vectra	11500
1996	Ford	Fiesta	7200
1995	Volkswagen	Polo	8500
1998	Ford	Mondeo	12000
1997	Renault	Clio	8000
1994	Seat	Swing	
1996	Nissan	Micra	
1993	Ford	Mondeo	

(a) Suggest a suitable General Purpose Package that would allow car dealers to prepare such an advertisement. Give a reason for your choice. **2**

(b) Newspaper staff re-type the details from a printout supplied by the car dealers. Car dealers offer to provide the information as an *ASCII* file on disc.

What is the benefit of using an ASCII file for data transfer? **2**

(c) The dealers use a spreadsheet package to produce their lists.

A discount of £250 is being offered on cars costing over £9000.

	A	B	C	D	E
1	**Year**	**Make**	**Model**	**Cost**	**SALE PRICE**
2	1996	Vauxhall	Vectra	11500	11250
3	1996	Ford	Fiesta	7200	7200
4	1995	Volkswagen	Polo	8500	8500
5	1998	Ford	Mondeo	12000	11750
6	1997	Renault	Clio	8000	8000

A formula in cell E2 is used to calculate the sale price. This formula has to be copied down the column.

Write down a suitable formula for E2 in this case. **3**

(d) The *cell attributes* of D2 to E6 are to be altered.

(i) What is meant by the term cell attributes? **1**

(ii) Suggest a suitable alteration to the cell attributes. **1**

(iii) Outline the steps required to make the alteration. **2**

	KU	PS

4. Laura buys a new computer from SmartPC.

(a) When Laura sends a document to her printer an error message appears on screen saying there is no *printer driver*.

What is a printer driver? **2**

(b) Laura phones SmartPC to enquire about a printer driver. They suggest she downloads it from their Internet Web Site.

The Internet is an example of a *Wide Area Network* (WAN). Laura's school has a *Local Area Network* (LAN).

Give **two** differences between a WAN and a LAN. **2**

(c) Internet hackers often break the *Computer Misuse Act*.

State **two** offences covered by this Act. **2**

(d) Laura is upgrading her computer for *multimedia* use.

Suggest **one** input device and **one** output device that she could buy to provide multimedia capabilities for her computer. **2**

(e) Multimedia presentations require the processing of large data files stored in RAM.

How does the CPU locate data stored in RAM? **2**

(f) One development in computer technology is *virtual reality*.

Virtual reality systems work in *real-time*.

(i) Why is it necessary to use a real-time operating system for virtual reality? **2**

(ii) Name an input device which can be used in virtual reality systems. **1**

	KU	PS

5. A soft drink manufacturer is considering changing the shape of its bottles. The bottle-making process uses an automated system with computer-controlled robots.

(a) The shape change may be possible because of the *adaptability* of the robots.

What is meant by the term adaptability? — KU 1

(b) The *end effector* is suitable for many of the tasks and the robot arms have the required *degrees of freedom* for the change.

   (i) What is an end effector? — KU 1

   (ii) What is meant by the term degrees of freedom? — KU 1

   (iii) Give one possible benefit of increasing the degrees of freedom. — PS 1

(c) The control systems make use of *ROM software*. The programs stored in ROM were written using a *control language*.

   (i) Why would programmers use a control language for this purpose? — PS 2

   (ii) State **two** advantages of having ROM software. — KU 2

(d) High level languages must be translated. Why is translation necessary? — KU 1

(e) State **two** advantages an interpreter has over a compiler. — PS 2

	KU	PS

6. Mix 'n' Match is an international pen pal agency. It stores information on members in a computer database. To register as a new member you have to complete an application form. A sample record is shown below.

Forename [   ]

Surname [   ]

Address [   ]

Country [   ]

Language [   ]

Date of Birth [ ][ ][ ][ ][ ][ ]
d d m m y y y y

(a) Suggest **two** additional fields and their data type. | | 2

(b) (i) Describe a *validation* check which should be performed on the **month** part of the Date of Birth. | 1 |

    (ii) What is the term used for this type of validation check? | 1 |

(c) The *screen input format* has the same layout as the application form. Why is this an advantage to the agency? | | 1

(d) The agency asks each applicant to send a passport-sized photograph with the form. Explain how the photograph could be included in the member's record. | | 2

(e) This database stores 500 000 records. Calculate the storage requirements, stating clearly any assumptions you make. | | 3

[END OF QUESTION PAPER]

NATIONAL
QUALIFICATIONS
2000

FRIDAY, 9 JUNE
2.35 PM – 4.20 PM

COMPUTING STUDIES
STANDARD GRADE
Credit Level

Read each question carefully.

Attempt **all** questions.

Write your answers in the answer book provided. **Do not** write on the question paper.

Write as neatly as possible.

Answer in sentences wherever possible.

	A	B	C	D	E	F
1			*Golf Shop Accounts 2000*			
2	**Rate of VAT**	**17·50%**				
3						
4	**Item**	**Each**	**Stock**	**Sub Total**	**VAT**	**Total**
5	Golf Balls	£1·25	200	£250·00	£43·75	£293·75
6	Golf Clubs	£65·00	30	£1950·00	£341·25	£2291·25
7	T'Shirts	£15·99	45	£719·55	£125·92	£845·47
8	Shorts	£11·99	65	£779·35	£136·39	£915·74
9	Socks	£3·99	500	£1995·00	£349·12	£2344·12
10	Sweaters	£19·99	50	£999·50	£174·91	£1174·41
11					Total	£7864·74

1. A golf club has a shop in which members can obtain many different types of goods. The shop uses a spreadsheet package to keep track of the goods it sells.

(a) (i) Spreadsheet formulae can use *relative referencing* or *absolute referencing*. Explain the term absolute referencing.

(ii) Name **two** columns which are likely to contain formulae.

(iii) Identify **one** cell which should contain an absolute reference. Explain your answer.

(b) *Cell protection* is a feature of spreadsheet software.

(i) What is meant by the term cell protection?

(ii) Suggest a column within this spreadsheet which should **not** be protected. Give **one** reason for your choice of column.

(c) The spreadsheet package can produce charts using *dynamic data linkage*. Explain what is meant by the term dynamic data linkage.

(d) The golf club would like to offer discounts to members. What function in a spreadsheet allows the user to handle problems which involve conditions?

(e) The golf club is thinking of setting up a *local area network* within the club so that both the shop and the club secretary can use the same customer database.

Describe **two** other benefits for the club of setting up a local area network.

KU	PS
2	
	2
	2
1	
	2
2	
1	
2	

	KU	PS

2. A school uses a computer system to analyse pupil performance in their recent tests. Each pupil fills in a record from a terminal in their classroom. Their data is updated each term. An example of part of a record is shown below.

| Name: | **ANGELA PLANK** | | | ID No: | 1 6 5 8 9 1 |

| Subjects | | | | | Grade |

	1	2	3	4	5	6	7
Art & Design	☒	☐	☐	☐	☐	☐	☐
Biology	☐	☒	☐	☐	☐	☐	☐
Chemistry	☐	☐	☐	☐	☐	☐	☐
Computing Studies	☐	☒	☐	☐	☐	☐	☐
English	☐	☒	☐	☐	☐	☐	☐

(a) (i) The classroom terminals are called *remote terminals*. What is a remote terminal? — KU **1**

   (ii) Each pupil is given a six-digit user identification number. The last digit is used to detect possible errors while entering a number. What name is given to this last digit? — KU **1**

(b) (i) When completed, the entry is processed immediately, and the pupil's average grade is displayed. What type of processing is this? — PS **1**

   (ii) What type of storage medium would the school use for this type of processing? Give a reason for your answer. — PS **2**

(c) The school has a large number of typed reports that it wishes to enter into the computer. One method is to use *optical character recognition* (OCR).

   Give **one** advantage and **one** disadvantage to the school of using OCR software to enter the data. — KU **2**

(d) A *range check* is one form of data validation. Give an example of a range check. — PS **2**

(e) Schools store other information about pupils. Suggest **two** ways in which data can be protected from unauthorised access. — KU **2**

	KU	PS

3. Mike manages a local sports club which has a maximum membership of 500. He uses a personal computer system which holds all the details of the club members on file.

On the first day of each month, Mike has to send a reminder to those members whose annual subscription is due that month. Standard letters are produced by using a word processing package. The personal details of the members are held in a database file.

(*a*) Here is an example of a membership record from the database.

Membership Number	5008
Title	Mr
Forename(s)	Arnold
Surname	Gallagher
Street	101 Redding Road
Town	Baconsville
Postcode	AN6 8GH
Telephone Number	0135 444 5053
Subscription Due	15/05/2000
Subscription Cost	20

An example of the standard letter sent out is shown below.

Mr Arnold Gallagher
101 Redding Road
Baconsville AN6 8GH
1 May 2000

Renewal of your annual subscription

Dear Arnold,
I see from our records that your annual subscription to the sports club is due on 15/05/2000. Your membership fee for next year will be £20.

Please complete the enclosed payment slip and send it back to me with your subscription.

Yours sincerely
Mike Hasselworth
Sports Club Manager

    (i) Which fields would be needed from Arnold's database record in order to send this personalised letter?

    (ii) Describe how Mike obtains the necessary data from the database for the standard letters in May.

   (iii) Describe how the personalised letters could be produced using the word processing package, assuming that the data required was saved in a file called *Renewals*.

	KU	PS
(i)		2
(ii)		4
(iii)		3

	KU	PS

(b) The word processor that Mike uses has a Graphical User Interface with *on-line help* and an *on-line tutorial*.

   (i) Give **one** example of a situation in which on-line help would be used. — KU: 1

   (ii) Give **one** example of a situation in which an on-line tutorial would be used. — KU: 1

(c) The sports club could use an integrated package to produce its personalised letters.

Give **two** advantages and **two** disadvantages of using an integrated package rather than separate packages for this task. — PS: 4

(d) Some people believe that they have the right to see **all** data held about them on a computer.

   (i) Give **one** argument for and **one** argument against this point of view. — KU: 2

   (ii) How does the Data Protection Act protect a person's rights? — KU: 2

	KU	PS

4. Rita Grant, the Principal Teacher of Computing Studies at High Academy, is looking for new computers for her computing department. She spotted the following two advertisements in a computer magazine.

ProGold

400 Mhz Processor
64Mb RAM
6·4Gb Hard Drive
1·44Mb 3·5" Floppy DD
4Mb Graphics Card
36 Speed CD ROM
16bit 3D sound Card
15" SVGA Monitor
Desktop Case

£798·95 ex VAT

ProGold Ultimate

500 Mhz Processor
128Mb RAM
6·4Gb Hard Drive
1·44Mb 3·5" Floppy DD
8Mb Graphics Card
Re-writeable optical disc
16bit 3D sound Card
17" SVGA Monitor
Tower Case

£898·95 ex VAT

(a) The ProGold Ultimate has a *re-writeable optical disc* drive rather than the *CD ROM disc* drive in the ProGold system. State **one** similarity and **one** difference between a re-writeable optical disc and a CD-ROM disc. — KU: **2**

(b) The ProGold system has 64Mb of memory. Describe how it is possible for a CPU to find a particular location in memory. — PS: **2**

(c) The ProGold Ultimate system is said to have *multi-access* and excellent *resource allocation*.

   (i) Explain the term multi-access. — KU: **1**

   (ii) Describe a situation where multi-access would be useful. — PS: **2**

   (iii) Explain the term resource allocation. — KU: **2**

(d) Both systems use a *hierarchical* filing system to store the data rather than a *flat* filing system. Give **one** advantage of each type of filing system. — KU: **2**

(e) All computer systems have a *Central Processing Unit* (CPU) containing an *Arithmetic & Logic Unit* (ALU) and a *Control Unit*. Explain the purpose of:

   (i) the Arithmetic & Logic Unit; — KU: **1**

   (ii) the Control Unit. — KU: **1**

(f) Both the ProGold and ProGold Ultimate systems are capable of running *multimedia* applications.

State **two** requirements of a computer system which would be needed to run multimedia applications. — KU: **2**

	KU	PS

5. Kensington's Knitwear Factory is thinking of expanding one of its manual production lines to include computer controlled knitting machines.

(a) A *systems analysis* is carried out before any new production line is built. Explain why a systems analysis is necessary. **2**

(b) The installation of the computer controlled knitting machines in the new production line would be *capital intensive*.

    (i) Why might the company consider spending large sums of money on this installation? **2**

    (ii) Give **one** disadvantage to employees of automation in the workplace. **1**

(c) The new knitting machines would use sensors to detect the position of the knitwear on the production line.

    (i) Why would this detection be useful? **1**

    (ii) What else would be needed to turn this into a closed loop system? **1**

(d) The specialised control software used in knitting machines may need to be changed frequently for new designs. What medium should be used to store the control software? Explain your answer. **2**

(e) The computer which runs the control software for the new production lines would use a *multi-programming* operating system.

    (i) What is meant by the term multi-programming? **2**

    (ii) Give **two** advantages of using multi-programming in this situation. **2**

[END OF QUESTION PAPER]

ANSWERS – GENERAL LEVEL 1996

1.   *(a)* Sort on name field in ascending order.
     (b) Search datafile in Next Service Due field for June 1996 **and** Car – Make & Model field for Volkswagen Polo.
     (c) (i)   Inaccurate information.
               Not kept secure. (others)
         (ii) Allow them to check (and correct) information held.
               Explain security arrangements. (others)
     (d) Takes up less space.
           Easier to sort records into order. (others)

2.   *(a)* Use cut and paste to cut the paragraph from original position and paste it into the new position.
     (b) Size of the dictionary, correct spelling, but the wrong context. (others)
     (c) Take a backup copy of her disc, and update it regularly.
     (d) Spreadsheet and word processor will have common HCI.
           Easier to transfer data between different packages without retyping. (others)
     (e) Make the drawings a different size, either larger or smaller.
     (f) It would improve the overall presentation of the report. (others)

3.   *(a)* (i)   Greater accuracy possible in the drawings.
               Easier to edit the drawings if something is changed. (others)
         (ii) Plotter.
         (iii) Fewer jobs, staff need to undergo training to work the system. (others)
     (b) (i)   Temperature sensor sends feedback signal to the computer so that it can adjust the heating as required.
         (ii) Heating could be on when it is not necessary.
         (iii) Control program in the computer was altered so that the heating switched off at a lower temperature.
         (iv) Automatic switching on/off of lights.
              Switching on/off air conditioning. (others)

4.   *(a)* (i)   =SUM(C2..C6)
         (ii) =C8-C6
     (b) Row 8 to replicate Passenger fares and row 10 for Profit.
     (c) Insert an extra row into the spreadsheet between rows 2 and 5.
     (d) (i)   The means by which the computer interacts with the user.
         (ii) Exact command can by typed in quickly. (others)

5.   *(a)* Small and convenient to carry. (others)
     (b) Modem
     (c) (i)   Sets her own work schedule.
                No travel costs. (others)
         (ii) More space for those still working in the office. (others)
         (iii) Less social contact between workers.

6.   *(a)* (i)   Quicker than entering purchases manually.
               Checkout operators do not need to know prices. (others)
         (ii) Check digit is a number added to the bar code to check that the correct number has been entered. It is calculated from the other numbers in the bar code.
     (b) (i)   Interactive processing is when processing takes place as soon as the input has been completed.
         (ii) Customers do not want to spend a long time at the checkout.

(c)   (i)   In case the card has been stolen.

       (ii)   Shop receives authorisation from the customer's bank for the transaction to go ahead.

(d)   (i)   Batch processing is when transactions are gathered together over a period of time to be processed all at once.

       (ii)   Can be done when the computer is not required for other things. (others)

(e)   (i)   Input details of the hours worked by the employees. (others)

       (ii)   Load the master files into the computer's memory. (others)

7.   (a)   File management.

        Input/Output control. (others)

    (b)   High level language looks like English. (others)

    (c)   (i)   10101011

            10001001

       (ii)   6 bytes to store this graphic.

    (d)   The number of different letters, numbers and symbols that the printer is able to print.

ANSWERS – GENERAL LEVEL 1997

1. *(a)* Sort the file on Name field into alphabetical (ascending) order and Print.
   (b) Field 1: Date of Purchase. Field 2: Make.
   (c) (i) Wide Area Network.
       (ii) Stock control.
           Electronic mail between shops and to and from Head Office. (others)
   (d) (i) Grant Electrical get paid for their lists. (others)
       (ii) Company knows everyone on the list has a video system. (others)
       (iii) Don't want a lot of junk mail arriving at their home. (others)

2. *(a)* =C7–C12
   (b) A range of cells is selected, starting with B12, and the formula is copied across to the other relevant cells.
   (c) The data has been formatted to show as currency.
   (d) A new column has been inserted between existing columns B and C.
   (e) (i) Touch sensitive screen.
       (ii) Don't need to have a keyboard to make any selections. (others)
   (f) (i) Don't have to type in same information each time — files are stored on disc.
           Appropriate paragraphs can be pulled into each customer's sheet as required. (others)
       (ii) A command can be directly typed in, no need to select from a number of menus. (others)
   (g) Paper for the printer.
       Discs for use with the system. (others)

3. *(a)* Easier to make changes to the report without having to retype it.
       Better presentation than a handwritten copy. (others)
   (b) (i) Checks his text against the words stored in the computer's dictionary and flags those words it doesn't find there. It offers alternatives, skip the words or to add them to the dictionary.
       (ii) Word which is used is the wrong word to use in the particular context, but is correctly spelled, e.g. "two" instead of "too".
       (iii) The spelling check may identify words which are not in its dictionary, particularly proper names or technical jargon, but are correctly spelled.
   (c) Alter top and/or bottom margins of the page. (others)
   (d) (i) Small and easy to carry around with him.
       (ii) Handwriting recognition.
       (iii) Liquid Crystal Display.
       (iv) (A) Search article for "Newport" and Replace with "Newtown".
           (B) Assistance which is called upon while working on the computer to explain how the various features work.

4. *(a)* Lessons which are available on the computer which teach you how to use the package.
   (b) Circle tool; Text tool. (others)
   (c) Alter line thickness; rotating graphic. (others)
   (d) Scanner could be used to input the logo into the computer.
   (e) Easier to switch between elements of integrated package, i.e. from drawing page to word processing page. (others)
   (f) The system could be operated via a password system. (others)

5. *(a)* Magnetic sensors on the bottom of the robot.
   (b) Sensors on the robot give feedback to the controlling computer which then decides on the next action.
   (c) Make the robots noisy.
       Make robots bright — either by colour or lights or both. (others)
   (d) No health problems for humans from the paint fumes.
       Robots can work without a break. (others)
   (e) Computer controlling the stationary robots has to be programmed on how to carry out the task.
   (f) Working conditions may be improved because there are fewer boring repetitive tasks to be done by the factory employees.

6.   *(a)*   To prove they are the authorised user of the card.
     (b)   MICR.
     (c)   (i)   Direct data entry.
           (ii)   Check that the bar code is valid by recalculating the check digit.   (others)
           (iii)   It is quicker to scan in the bar code which brings up the price than have to make sure that all goods have price tickets on them.   (others)
     (d)   (i)   Doesn't have to carry much money around with him.   (others)
           (ii)   Shop doesn't have as much money lying around in the safe.   (others)
     (e)   Details are processed as soon as the computer receives them.
     (f)   All details are collected together and then processed as one 'batch' of the same thing at a later time.

7.   *(a)*   (i)   CD ROM would be used where you simply wanted to review information.   (others)
           (ii)   Hard disc would be used where you wanted to be able to make changes to information.   (others)
     (b)   1   File management.
          2   Input/Output control.   (others)
     (c)   High level languages use words which are similar to English.
         One high level language instruction generates several machine code instructions.   (others)
     (d)   Character set is the letters, numbers and symbols which the printer is able to print.
     (e)   (i)   A real time system reacts immediately to changes in the temperature.
           (ii)   Another real time system would be a security system.   (others)

1. *(a)* (i) Word Processing.
        (ii) Spreadsheet.

    (b) Find/Change, Search and Replace.

    (c) 1. Does not have scientific words in its dictionary.
        2. Will ignore words spelt correctly but misused.

    (d) (i) Scanner.
        (ii) Able to store the image.

    (e) Scale graphic.

    (f) 1. Working disc could get damaged.
        2. Working disc could get lost.

2. *(a)* Sort on field Surname.

    (b) Search; Amount owed < 100.   And; Last Order > 1st January, 1998.

    (c) (i) To prevent somebody looking at the screen from finding out the password.
        (ii) To restrict access to authorised persons only.

    (d) (i) 1. Easy to search.   2. Produce reports.
        (ii) 1. Initial cost of hardware, etc.   2. Training costs.
        (iii) Maintenance of hardware.

3. *(a)* (i) C3 * D3.
        (ii) E3 + B3.

    (b) (i) Contents of one cell are copied into another and the formulae automatically adjust for the new row or column.
        (ii) Formula in cell F3 could be replicated in F4..F6.

    (c) Alter attributes to currency.

    (d) Available as a pull-down menu giving further choice of commands for help and which can be accessed while program is in use.

    (e) Takes the user step-by-step through a program demonstrating its features.

4. *(a)* To prevent unauthorised access.

    (b) (i) Program which interacts with user.
        (ii) It is used as result is required without delay.

    (c) (i) Data is collected and fed into computer and once stored there is no human intervention until process is finished.
        (ii) Other tasks can be done during the day.

    (d) (i) 1. No need to carry cash.   2. Faster than writing cheques
        (ii) 1. Less chance of theft as less cash collected.   2. Less paperwork.

5. *(a)* Has a built-in map which it uses to determine the shortest route.

    (b) It is fitted with sensors which give a feedback when people or objects are detected.

    (c) Interacting with a computer program and receiving output immediately.

    (d) (i) Nurses can spend more time looking after their patients.
        (ii) Loss of nursing jobs.

    (e) 1. Cost of purchasing.   2. Maintenance costs.

    (f) Can only perform one task.

6. *(a)* 1. Check input devices.   2. Manages the filing system.

   (b) A system which uses icons.

   (c) Ease of use.

   (d) 1. Easier to edit.   2. More like English.

   (e) (i) Accessibility by a disabled person.
        (ii) The disabled person could have difficulty in operating a keyboard.

   (f) (i) Where writing can be turned into print.
        (ii) The text can be imported into a word processor.

7. *(a)* Improve image of company.

   (b) Modem.

   (c) 1. Transferring of data.   2. E-mail service between stations.

   (d) (i) Less time wasted travelling to office.
        (ii) Increased sales.

   (e) CD ROM can hold vast amount of data.

   (f) LCD needs little power to operate it.

1. *(a)* This type of computer is portable.
   (b) Alter line length, change page length.
   (c) Help in the form of information screens available when using a computer program.
   (d) Transfer data and programs between computers.
       E-mail between computers on the network.
   (e) Menu driven systems are usually more user-friendly than command-driven systems.
   (f) A graphical user interface has icons or pictures.

2. *(a)* Sort on field name.
   (b) (i) Course; gender.   (ii) Wordprocessing.
   (c) Use of passwords.
       Doors to rooms containing storage media and computer systems must be kept locked.
   (d) Only authorised personnel allowed to work on computer system.
   (e) Yes. Data Protection Act allows her to see a copy of her personal data.

3. *(a)* (i) = B4 + C4 + D4.   (ii) = B4 + B7 + B10 + B13.
   (b) (i) Replicated means that the formulae will be copied and will automatically change to suit the position.
       (ii) Formulae in B18 replicated in C18 and D18.
   (c) Insert additional rows and add new data.
   (d) Charting.

4. *(a)* (i) Bar code.
       (ii) Country of origin; name; price.
       (iii) Range check.
       (iv) Scanner shows what you have spent.
       (v) LCD is a flat display device.
   (b) (i) Obtain a brief statement; transfer money between accounts.
       (ii) The PIN is the customer's password to the computer system.
   (c) (i) Magnetic ink characters.
       (ii) Time delay in the supermarket getting the money; cheque might bounce.
   (d) Batch processing involves data being handled in one set.

5. *(a)* Checks input devices like keyboard and mouse; manages the filing system.
   (b) HLL programs are easier to read and write because the instructions are written in everyday language.
       HLL should help the programmer solve problems.
   (c) (i) RAM.
       (ii) A program is a list of instructions and when run can produce or use a data file.
   (d) (i) No. Operating system requires two megabytes which leaves only 6 MB of main memory.
       (ii) Adding extra main memory will allow user to run larger programs and keep more data in memory. This makes
           the computer system work faster because it is quicker to access data from main memory than from disk.
   (e) Advantage: no need to load software from disk every time the computer is switched on.
       Disadvantage: difficult to upgrade software.

6. *(a)* Working in space, hazardous environment.
       Robotic arm can be re-programmed to do different tasks.
   (b) A closed loop is a system which uses feedback. The computer then reacts to that feedback to alter the output.
   (c) (i) Using CAD, a picture on a computer screen can be turned around and viewed from any angle.
           CAD system can greatly reduce the amount of work a designer has to do by making all the necessary
           calculations.
       (ii) Input device: digitising tablet. Output device: plotters.

7. (a) Modem.
        Communications package.
    (b) Wide area network.
    (c) Accessing data on other computer systems; use of e-mail.
    (d) (i) Able to work to his own timetable.
              No travelling expenses.
         (ii) Feeling of isolation.

ANSWERS COMPUTING STUDIES — GENERAL LEVEL 2000

1. (a) Use standard paragraphs.
   (b) Use search and replace for the phrase 'The Scottish Office'. Identify replacement 'The Scottish Parliament'.
   (c) Letters of the alphabet, numbers, special characters.
   (d) Spell checker.
   (e) A person's name.
   (f) There and their.
   (g) Handwriting recognition.
   (h) Portability of system.

2. (a) (i) Search the database on the fields. Guitar = Electric. Cost < £300.
        (ii) The stock field will show that there are more than zero available.
   (b) (i) Altered the record format.
        (ii) Printed output.
   (c) (i) Set of instructions for computer to follow.
        (ii) A file containing data used by a program.

3. (a) Like English to read. Easier to correct if errors occur.
   (b) Machine code.
   (c) Scanner.

4. (a) (i) Training costs. Initial costs of system.
        (ii) They don't have such a high wage bill.
   (b) (i) Sensor detecting light reflected. Sensor detecting light not reflected. Providing feedback from sensors to computer controlling motors.
        (ii) Use of barriers. Use of lights flashing to warn of a robot's approach.
   (c) People don't get hurt if things go wrong.
   (d) Speed of response.

5. (a) (i) A command driven system is less user friendly.
        (ii) Graphical User Interface.
   (b) (i) Set of tasks the user works through to gain familiarity with a package.
        (ii) A feature that allows the user to find out about the operation of a package that can be used during the use of the package.
   (c) Scale and rotate.
   (d) Local Area Network.
   (e) Centre the text.
   (f) Fewer people in the office and therefore more space available per person and also quieter.
   (g) Control of access, e.g., passwords.
   (h) (i) The police.
        (ii) It could prevent the police from doing their job.

6. (a) Replicate the formula from E2 into cells E3 to E5.
   (b) (i) Insert a row between the information on row 4 and row 5.
        (ii) Alter the column width.
   (c) Alter the cell attributes.

7. (a) (i) Discusses how a company might want to replace manual jobs with computer systems and decides if this is possible.
        (ii) Provides maintenance for computer systems.
   (b) (i) Electronic Funds Transfer.
        (ii) Guaranteed payment.
        (iii) No need to carry money around.
   (c) Wide Area Network.
   (d) Ink jet printer gives better quality.
   (e) Spreadsheet.
   (f) File handling. Handling input devices.

8. (a) To allow user to "talk" to computer system.
   (b) Other people can hear your personal information being spoken to you.
   (c) Difficulty in system understanding different people's voices.
   (d) (i) Magnetic Ink Character Recognition.
        (ii) Less chance of error being made in processing the cheque. Faster to process the cheques than by hand.
   (e) Liquid Crystal Display.
   (f) Information is data set in a structure and context.

1. (a) (i)   Document reader will be used.
      (ii) Quicker than typing in choices; fewer mistakes during input stage. (others)
   (b) (i)   To give each pupil a unique number.
      (ii) Makes sure that numbers input are valid.
   (c) Cards are all done at one time; computer system not taken up with task on interactive basis.
   (d) A range check that values are between 1 and 12.
   (e) Transaction file has to be sorted into the same order as the pupil master file.

2. (a) (i)   An interface which uses icons to represent files on screen.
      (ii) Static data link where a change to data in one part of the package will not show up in an associated part.
   (b) (i)   Track Number 3 bytes; Title 13 bytes; Artist 23 bytes; Playing time 4 bytes
            Total for one record 3 + 13 + 23 + 4 = 43 bytes
      (ii) 43 bytes multiplied by 2000 = 86000/1024 = 83.984 Kbytes.
   (c) Search for Artist field containing Michael and the Bandits **and** Playing Time less than 4 minutes. Resulting answer then sorted into ascending order of Track Number.
   (d) Register with the Data Protection Registrar.
   (e) Create word processed letter with place markers for variable information, have datafile which contains variable information, merge two files together to produce personalised letters.

3. (a) Compiles program runs faster than interpreted.
       Once compiled, the translator program does not need to be present on the computer. (others)
   (b) Software is portable if it can be run on a different type of machine from the machine which originally created it.
   (c) (i)   Multi-access – many users able to access the computer at the same time.
      (ii) Travel agents accessing a central booking system for flights, holidays, etc. (others)
   (d) (i)   Hierarchical filing system.
      (ii) Files can be stored with the same name, if in different directories, e.g. ex 1.
            Similar types of programs may be stored together, e.g. GPP or Personal.
   (e) Arithmetic and Logic Unit.
   (f) May be held as mantissa (832.471) and exponent (3).
   (g) (i)   Ease of communication between computer and peripheral devices like printers. (others)
      (ii) VDU 2; VDU 3. (others)

4. (a) (i)   Open loop system because there is no feedback.
      (ii) Sensors would provide feedback to the computer enabling lights to respond to the volume of traffic.
      (iii) Movement sensor. (others)
   (b) (i)   Decide what tasks may be automated; design the new system. (others)
      (ii) Number of ways in which robot arm is able to move.
      (iii) Computer is only able to understand digital input.
   (c) (i)   Easy to upgrade disc based software. (others)
      (ii) Quicker to load up than disc based software. (others)

5. (a) (i)   C5 * D5
      (ii) Relative referencing as formula changes as it is copied down the column.
      (iii) Cell protection prevents cell being changed accidentally.
   (b) (i)   Virtual reality where the computer represents a 3-D image of reality for the user.
      (ii) Virtual reality headset. (others)

6. (a) Modem; communications software. (others)
   (b) Access to databases of information on Internet; use e-mail facilities to contact other children. (others)
   (c) (i)   Government agencies/departments. (others)
      (ii) Register with the group; receive password to use in future.
   (d) Computer Misuse Act 1990.

1.   (a)   Computer may not be able to cope with graphics.
              Disc format may not be suitable.   (others)
  (b)   Separate packages more expensive than integrated package.
              May take up more memory than integrated package.   (others)
  (c)   (i)   Letter whose content stays largely the same throughout, only small parts will change.
        (ii)   Database.
        (iii)   Printer driver is the software program which allows her printer to work with the computer.
  (d)   (i)   A cell is the box which is the intersection of a column and a row.
        (ii)   Cells are locked so that data cannot be accidentally overwritten.

2.   (a)   A computed field has an answer worked out from a formula which refers to other fields in the database.
  (b)   (i)   A row.
        (ii)   A column.
  (c)   (i)   (A)   (B7 + C7)/2
                 (B)   (B5 + C5)/2
        (ii)   Relative replication.

3.   (a)   (i) $20 + 4 + 8 + 1 + 1 + 1 + 1 = 36$ bytes
        (ii) $720Kb = 720*1024 = 737\ 280$ bytes
            Number of records $= 737\ 280/36 = 20\ 480$
  (b)   **Search** the database for **class** containing 2T1F **and overall grade** less than 3.
  (c)   (i)   Pupil field needs to show surname before initial.
        (ii)   Database should be **sort**ed on **overall grade and pupil**, both in ascending order.
  (d)   Use menu driven rather than command driven.
              Use on-line help for pupils.   (others)
  (e)   (i)   Register with Data Protection Registrar.
        (ii)   The pupils are the data subjects.

4.   (a)   Country of origin and manufacturer may be in the bar code.   (others)
  (b)   Price and number in stock may be held on the central computer.   (others)
  (c)   (i)   To ensure that the bar code has been read correctly by the bar code reader.
        (ii)   Bar code is read by computer. It recalculates the check digit and compares with the check digit on the bar code. If both are the same, chances are the bar code is correct.
  (d)   Poor handwriting may lead to errors on the OCR forms.
  (e)   Palmtops can be used for direct entry to the central computer.
              Handwriting is not so important.   (others)
  (f)   Typed in by two different people and entries compared.
              Typist asked to check each entry before continuing.

5.   (a)   Work is carried out by human operators.
  (b)   Production would have increased.
              Robots can work for longer periods without making errors.   (others)
  (c)   An attachment which is part of a robot arm to let it do a different task.
  (d)   Software cannot be lost when computer is switched off.
              Software can be loaded up quicker than disc-based.   (others)
  (e)   Heating could be reduced.
              Canteen and other staff facilities could be left out of the design.   (others)
  (f)   System analysis examines the tasks being done to see if robots could do them, and to make recommendation regarding hardware and software.

6.   (a)   (i)   Payroll would use sequential access because all records would be read in turn.
        (ii)   Stock control would use direct access because records have to be updated immediately.
  (b)   A number of different programs can be run by the mainframe at the same time.

7.   (a)   CD ROM and stereo speakers.   (others)
  (b)   (i)   An assembler translates assembly mnemonics into machine code.
        (ii)   Both are translators.   (others)
  (c)   The number of bits the computer is able to process at one time.
  (d)   (i)   Make use of standard character sets like ASCII.
        (ii)   Printer has a different code for £.
        (iii)   To switch the printer on and to switch the printer off.   (others)

1. *(a)* (i) Common HCI and ease of transfer of data.
   (ii) May use more memory.
   (b) Dynamic linkage — so that when the change is made in the spreadsheet, it will be transferred automatically to the graph.
   (c) (i) A letter which is the same over and over again with parts which are personalised.
   (ii) A standard letter involves typing out a master copy, with fixed information. Having a data file, with all the variable data and merging these to produce the standard letters.
   (d) (i) It compares the words which have been entered with the words in its dictionary.
   (ii) Sea and see, their and there.
   (e) (i) A printer driver.
   (ii) Bold, italics.

2. *(a)* (i) The part that fits on the end of the arm.
   (ii) Gripper.
   (b) (i) The number of ways the arm can move.
   (ii) 1 degree of freedom.
   (c) (i) Speed of loading.
   (ii) Easier to upgrade.
   (d) (i) Open Loop — there are no sensors.
   (ii) It could sense when the grip was tight enough and send a signal back to stop closing.

3. *(a)* Software.
   (b) Disabled.
   (c) (i) The cells can be protected.
   (ii) C8 * D8.
   (iii) Absolute referencing. VAT is fixed, so the value in cell B3 should always be used.
   (iv) An extra row would be added.
   (d) (i) The database would have 2000 records.
   (ii) Computed field.
   (iii) Colour of text; command driven; size of text.
   (iv) An extra record would be added.

4. *(a)* A word is the number of bits that can be processed in a single operation.
   (b) Compiler, interpreter.
   (c) (i) Where directories can hold files.

   (ii) Easier to find files. Files can be organised by subject.
   (d) Binary digit.
   (e) (i) Arithmetic Unit. Control Unit.
   (ii) Control Unit controls all the activity of the CPU. Arithmetic Unit carries out the calculations.

5. *(a)* (i) Magnetic tape.
   (ii) Floppy disc.
   (iii) She should use disc because random access will be quicker than sequential access.
   (b) (i) To check on the accuracy of the data.
   (ii) It could be entered twice.
   (c) Bar codes — they would tend to be read as the item was issued, rather than kept together and processed as a batch.
   (d) (i) File ancestry means keeping the previous versions.
   (ii) Three generations are kept because it reduces the chances of losing data, while two generations would be too few.

6. *(a)* Speak into a microphone.
   (b) (i) Helmet monitor.
   (ii) Playing a game to provide stimulation.
   (c) Suitable for some disabilities such as for the blind. Doesn't require expensive output devices.

1. (a) A device used for on-line data entry to a computer.
    (b) (i)   System that supports many users on an interactive basis.
         (ii) Many sales assistants require immediate response to stock enquiries.
    (c) A modem and telephone line.
    (d) (i)   Use backup copy of the transaction file.
               Use previous day's master file and transaction file to recreate lost master file.
    (e) Optical character reader.
    (f) Maximise CPU use, e.g., overnight when not required interactively.
         No interaction required.

2. (a) Register intent with DP Registrar.
    (b) (i)   Search the file on fields; total loan > = 10 000 and loan paid off = "yes".
         (ii) Document format is already printed with boxes for details that change.
               Printing time is faster since not printing complete document.
         (iii) Database is searched for required lucky customers.
               Letter file contains markers in required position.
               Personal details found above is merged with standard letter file to produce personalised letter.
    (c) Alter record format to include a computed field with suitable fieldname — amount remaining.
         Period of loan — payment to date × monthly payment.
    (d) (i)   Immediate access required to files.
         (ii) Backup does not require immediate access.
    (e) (i)   Data Protection Act.
         (ii) Check data for accuracy.
         (iii) Must register.

3. (a) Word processor — allows columns of text.
    (b) ASCII is a standard format that can be produced by most GPP and reads most others without special translators.
    (c) E2 = IF(D2 > 9000, D2 – 250, D2).
    (d) (i)   Formatting applied to the cell.
         (ii) Alter to currency (£).
         (iii) Select cells D2–E6: choose to format cells.

4. (a) A program that allows the computer to print to a particular type of printer.
    (b) WAN — requires telephone / modem / other link.
         LAN — data transfer rates higher than WAN.
    (c) To gain unauthorised access to a computer system and to make changes to data.
    (d) Input — video camera.
         Output — speakers.
    (e) Every location in memory has a unique address.
    (f) (i)   Processing of inputs has to be instantaneous to allow the events to be as realistic as possible.
         (ii) Dataglove.

5. (a) Can be set different types of task.
    (b) (i)   Tool fitted to the end of a robot arm.
         (ii) Number of independent movements.
         (iii) An increase in DOF will allow for more intricate types of task.
    (c) (i)   Commands and syntax, more suited to the task.
         (ii) Cannot be erased accidentally or deliberately.
               Difficult to copy.
    (d) Computer operates in machine code.
    (e) Mistakes corrected at time of entry.
         Syntax errors reported immediately.

6. (*a*) Postcode; text.
  (*b*) (i) To ensure number lies within sensible range.
    (ii) Range check.
  (*c*) Fields are positioned on screen in same position as on form.
  (*d*) A scanner could be used and the image positioned into the record.
  (*e*) Data   = 180 bytes
    × 500 000   = 90 000 000 bytes
    / 1000 : 1024 = 90 000 k = 90 Mb

ANSWERS — CREDIT LEVEL 2000

1. *(a)* (i) Absolute referencing — when a formula has to be copied exactly as it is from one cell to another, i.e., the cell reference stays constant.
       (ii) Columns D or E.
       (iii) E5 — The reference to cell B2 must remain constant when the formula is replicated down column E.
    (b) (i) Cell protection is where information in cells are locked or protected from being altered.
       (ii) Column C — Stock may need to be changed regularly.
    (c) Dynamic data linkage means that if you use the same data in different parts of the package, i.e., spreadsheet and graphics, and you change the data in one package, the change will automatically be carried out in the other package.
    (d) Conditional function.
    (e) Sharing of expensive peripherals; communication between shop and secretary.

2. *(a)* (i) A terminal where data is entered which is not in the same room or even the same building as the computer processing the data.
       (ii) A check digit.
    (b) (i) Interactive processing.
       (ii) Hard disc; immediate access.
    (c) Advantage — a large amount of data can be loaded into a word processor by people without typing skills.
       Disadvantage — errors in scanning.
    (d) Grades 1 to 7.
    (e) Passwords, security cards.

3. *(a)* (i) <Title>, <Forename>, <Surname>, <Street>, <Town>, <Postcode>, <Subscription Due> and <Subscription Cost> fields.
       (ii) Search the database on the <Subscription Due> field for the dates which lie between 01/05/2000 AND 31/05/2000.
       (iii) Create a standard letter in the word processing package with the space for details in the appropriate places. Use the file Renewals to start a mail merge to insert the database headings into the letter at the appropriate places. Start the mail merge by printing the letters.
    (b) (i) Where the paper manuals were not provided.
       (ii) When the user requires to be told step-by-step how to perform a particular operation, without looking up the paper manuals.
    (c) Advantages — Exchange of data, less sophisticated features to learn.
       Disadvantages — Less features than necessary, new packages to learn.
    (d) (i) For — up-to-date information.   Against — restriction of information held.
       (ii) Not to be used for any reason incompatible with its original purpose; be made available to the individual concerned and provision made for correction.

4. *(a)* Both have data read to them by laser beams but rewriteable discs can have their contents changed whereas CD-ROM discs cannot.
    (b) Main memory is divided into individual storage locations and each location has a unique number or address.
    (c) (i) Multi-access — A number of terminals connected to the processor with the processor time shared between many users.
       (ii) Airline reservations.
       (iii) Resource allocation — the OS decides what resources are connected to the CPU. These are allocated according to the requirements of the programs. They are connected and disconnected from the CPU as different resources are required.
    (d) Advantage hierarchical — Organisation of files and directories, same name can be used for files as long as they are in different directories.
       Advantage flat — Very simple to use and easy to find files.
    (e) (i) Arithmetic and Logic Unit — performs all the arithmetical and logical operations on any data passed to the processor.
       (ii) Control Unit — supervises the execution of the program instructions inside the processor.
    (f) Great deal of memory, large hard discs.

5. *(a)* To ensure that the manual tasks can be transferred to a computerised system, effectively and efficiently.
    (b) (i) Long-term savings.
       (ii) Loss of jobs.
    (c) (i) To identify if the knitwear is in the correct position.
       (ii) Feedback.
    (d) Any recordable media such as CD-R or disc — the information can therefore be updated when required.
    (e) (i) This means that a number of different programs are running at the same time on a single computer.
       (ii) One machine could be knitting a new design while another is being printed out.

NOTES

NOTES

Printed by Bell & Bain Ltd., Glasgow, Scotland.